Get Rich Off A Minimum Wage Income!

Kevin McNeely, MBA

This publication is designed to provide accurate and authoritative information in regard to the subject matter covered. It is sold with the understanding that the publisher or author is not engaged in rendering legal, accounting, or other professional service. If legal advice or other expert assistance is required, the services of a competent professional person should be sought.

Editor: Kevin McNeely

Cover Design: Kevin McNeely

Typesetting: Kevin McNeely

© 2011 by Kevin McNeely

Self published by Kevin McNeely

All rights reserved. The text of this publication, or any part thereof, may not be reproduced in any manner whatsoever without the written permission from the publisher or author.

Printed in the United States of America

Dedication

This is dedicated to Summer and Christian. I love you both so much. Thank you for supporting me over the years as we moved together through this crazy adventure we call life.

Foreword

Most people who never achieve their dreams are not held back by difficult circumstances. They are not stopped by lack of opportunity or because strong men oppose them. They fail simply because they don't believe they can succeed.

-Pat Williams

Quite often I drive the streets of my adopted home town in Copperas Cove, Texas and I take in the picturesque landscape. I marvel at the rolling hills and beautiful dwarf trees dotting the countryside. The beauty of hill country in central Texas is exactly why I chose this location for my retirement following a successful military career.

As I drive down the street from my middle class neighborhood with its newly constructed ranch and split-level homes I gaze in awe at the massive American flag flying freely over my housing division. It causes me to reflect on my own story. It is a story deeply rooted in the American dream.

I was raised in a dysfunctional household in the ghettos of Los Angeles. My mom was a single parent who had multiple kids by multiple men. She freely used drugs in front of me and my siblings. She exposed us to drug lords and gangs. It is no surprise my other siblings went on to live lackluster lives.

However there isn't any difference between my siblings and me. We share the same genes. I went on to graduate from college, own several pieces of real estate and become a commissioned officer in military while my siblings lived their lives mostly on public assistance struggling for the scraps of what society had to offer.

As I reflect on my story it pains me to realize my story is not unique. It is a story being rewritten and rewritten. As I continue my drive, I pass two churches. After passing the second church I enter the lower economic neighborhoods. I look at the worn, old homes. I take in the peeling paint and dilapidated windows and I imagine chilly drafts creeping in under the window sills on crisp Texas winter nights. I know in some of those homes my story is being rewritten and this bothers me.

This is why I wrote this book. I want this story to stop. I want the final chapter of this tale of poverty to end with me. I sigh to myself because I fear it's probably not likely but it's definitely worth a shot anyway. Maybe I can reach a few people. Perhaps one or two people will change their lives by reading this book. If that occurs I consider it a major victory and well-worth the countless hours I've spent reading and researching to create this book.

Introduction

He that returns a good for evil obtains the victory.

-Thomas Fuller

The Lack of Money is the Root of all Evil

Some say money is the root of all evil. I argue the lack of money is. I'm borrowing this argument from Robert Kiyosaki the author of "Rich Dad, Poor Dad." Let's think about this. Those who demonstrate anti-social behavior are normally poor. Yes, there are some exceptions but let's look at the majority of instances. When was the last time you saw a "COPS" episode with a kicking and screaming guy in a business suit being arrested? When was the last time an entire episode was dedicated to patrolling middle class neighborhoods and roughing up middle class citizens?

You haven't seen episodes of "COPS" or "Bait Car" in middle class neighborhoods because crime is rare there. Of course it happens from time to time but statistically there is a big difference between crime rates in lower economic areas opposed to higher ones.

People do unholy things when they lack money. This is a documented fact in history and it'll continue in the future. The only solution to crime is to combat poverty and the battle starts today. Contrary to popular opinion, poverty is a choice. We must influence those to choose wealth over poverty. Poverty isn't linked to income either; it is linked to choices.

This book explores how we can make lasting changes in our society, our communities and ourselves with even a small income. The road to riches is unobstructed. All can walk down its path. All it takes is self-reflection, self-discovery, desire and a commitment to change. I know you have what it takes in you. I feel your potential and it is great. But no one can do it for you. Your first steps to wealth and change begins here with this book. If you practice its teaching you can change yourself and you can help change the world.

Chapter 1

Our greatest wealth is not measured in terms of riches but relationships.

-Oliver Cromwell

What is wealth?

Many people have a false perception of what wealth is. They incorrectly define wealth in material stuff. This fallacy is often instigated by the media. The media flocks to stories of Americans living lavish lifestyles. They'll show some TV personality or some popular music icon jetting around the country in a private jet.

They'll show a popular professional skater freely purchasing and fulfilling all his desires. Homes, contemporary furniture, hot tubs, gold plated cars with state-of-the art stereo systems all define wealth for many Americans. The theme is the same. Your wealth is defined by what you own and consume but this is so far from the truth.

Here is where I challenge you to think differently. I challenge you to open your eyes and see what wealth really is. The real truth is most of these people living these lifestyles are far from wealthy. They struggle living paycheck to paycheck. The difference is their paychecks are just larger. I know what you are thinking now. You are asking yourself if they aren't wealthy, if these icons do not define wealth, then what does? The answer may surprise you.

Wealth is simply stored money. This is significantly different from spent money. Spent money is how most Americans perceive wealth to be. Spent money is what the media perceives wealth to be and spent money is the worst way to define wealth.

Consider this, if money is spent, it is not renewable. It is simply gone but if money is STORED, it is renewable. Stored money is the way the rich get richer and spent money is why the working class continues to struggle.

I listen to people struggling to improve themselves financially. It is the same, old song. They'll say things like "If only I can make more cash" or "Once I get my degree, I'll make some real green." These statements are flawed. More money will only result in them spending more. I'm here to say financial independence is achievable with any income! Let me say that again because it is important that this statement sinks in. Financial independence is achievable with any income!

I know I created doubters and skeptics with that statement. I know a lot of you are ready to close this book and ignore the wisdom I'm going to present to you but I encourage you to resist that feeling. I implore you to approach everything I have to say with an open mind because it could be life changing.

In future chapters I'll go into the specifics on how to build wealth with any income but for now I'm going to introduce to you to a critical concept. I want you to know this, there is a DIFFERENCE between wealth and income. Hmmmmm, how so?

In earlier paragraphs we talked about what wealth is. We defined it as stored money. So isn't wealth and income the same? Aren't high income earners wealthy? The answer is maybe. High income earners can be wealthy or they cannot be. The answer of whether or not they are wealthy depends on how much money they actually store away from their monthly incomes. If they store a lot of it consistently; they are probably wealthy. If they store none of it; they surely are not wealthy. The world is loaded with high income earners that aren't wealthy. Let's look at a case study.

You all remember a football player by the name of Michael Vick right? He was a blessed athlete and he commanded a large salary in the NFL. During the height of his career he was making millions annually. Surely this guy was wealthy right? Not exactly. To make a long story short he got involved in illegal dog fighting and was sent to jail but here's the kicker. Abandoned by the NFL and cut off from his multiple million dollar salary, Michael Vick eventually filed for bankruptcy.

Despite being paid millions of dollars over the span of his career, he was virtually penniless. Why? He spent it all. Michael Vick did not store money so he was not, is not wealthy. I have to admit that at the time of this writing Michael Vick's story is still unfinished. He emerged from prison and was reinstated with the NFL. His salary is a small fraction of what it once was though but his ability to become wealthy is not about the amount of his income; it's about what he does with it.

In a 2009 article from the Associated Press, Michael Vick still owes about $20 million in debts to various creditors. He has plans to liquidate some of his homes, boats and high-end sports utility vehicles to satisfy these debts and rebuild his reputation. Now let's look at me.

In 1992 I entered the military as an Airman Basic. I was at the bottom of the totem pole. I was paid about

$720.60 a month. Since I was paid every two weeks I made a whopping $360.30 per paycheck. As the years have passed I've gotten some promotions and pay raises but I haven't made nearly as much as Michael Vick. I'm only 38 years old now and I've amassed hundreds of thousands in cash and assets. My story is very different from his and I'm probably wealthier than he is. I can proudly say I've never filed for bankruptcy and I have no plans to file in the future.

My story is a real example of the difference between income and wealth. I've accumulated close to a half a million dollars on a working man's salary and I did it by storing money.

I have to admit that I've never made minimum wage. My salary has always been slightly higher than that but I have helped minimum wage earners accumulate serious wealth with my action plan and if you make minimum wage or more; I can help you too. The first step towards accumulating wealth begins not at the bank or some flashy investment company. It begins with you. You have to understand your desires and control them.

Chapter 2

The secret of success is constancy of purpose.

-Benjamin Disraeli

What Are Desires?

One of my favorite websites, Dictionary.com defines desire as "to wish or long for; crave; want." It goes on to provide another definition "a longing or craving, as for something that brings satisfaction or enjoyment." My thoughts are these definitions kind of hit the mark but I still see weaknesses. I have particular beef with the second definition above. It's really the last part of the definition that I think is faulty. I do not feel any desire can bring LASTING satisfaction or enjoyment. Let me expand on why I feel this way.

I feel desires are in a way like addictive drugs. I feel when you satisfy one desire, you'll immediately want more. Just like addictive drugs, satisfying desires can be self-destructive. Now let me be clear I'm not saying you should go through life not getting anything you want. What I'm saying is you must control your desires and NOT let your desires control you. This is what happened to Michael Vick. He let his desires control him.

In 2011 I read a fascinating book by Robert Kiyosaki and it really changed my thinking about a lot of things. In a sense it changed my life and I recommend that after you finish reading my book; you rush out and buy a copy of his.

In his book he wrote a story about a donkey and a carrot. The moral of the story had something to do with the illusion of money. I won't go into detail about what that means because he can explain it better than I can but for some strange reason the picture of a donkey latched to a cart stuck with me. In his book he painted a picture with words that showed a farmer sitting in a cart that was latched to this donkey. The farmer held a pole. Tied to the pole was a carrot. The carrot lazily dangled in front of the donkey. The donkey would steadily labor to get to the carrot pulling the cart along but the carrot was always just out of reach. Mr. Kiyosaki goes on to call the carrot an illusion.

I totally agree with his assessment and I tie this story into fulfilling desires. When one tries to fulfill one's desires, it is more of an illusion than a reality because when you fulfill one desire; it is quickly replaced by another. Think about that for a while and think about your own situation. Think about your own life. Think about the material possessions you longed for and fulfilled. Did it completely satisfy your desires? Meaning, did you never long for anything again? Of course not, one desire was quickly replaced by another one, wasn't it? That's why I feel fulfilling desires is an illusion. I really don't think you can satisfy all your desires in a lifetime.

I recall many years ago I lived in a sleepy town in Oklahoma. It was nestled in the northwest corner of the state. It was a windy place as I recall it with harsh winters and hot summers. It always felt like I was walking into a hair dryer outside on summer afternoons.

One day I saw this cool looking dude on a sweet crotch rocket. It was a sleek machine with aesthetic colors. I imagined women would flock to a guy like that if he pulled up to a nightclub on that machine. You see, Enid's economy was largely centered on the local Air Force base and I sized up that guy to be a pilot. He was probably a future fighter pilot. I perceived him to be cocky and attitudinal. It's funny how flawed we are, isn't it? We make judgments on people without even knowing them.

So immediately I desired a motorcycle. I wanted to be cool and sleek like that guy. I wanted women to long for me. I wanted to feel like I was the man. I was very frugal by this time and I had a sizable saving so I decided to treat myself to a bike. But I had one problem I didn't know how to ride one and I was terrified of the thought of shifting gears.

So I compromised with myself. I settled on a motor scooter but before you laugh this was one powerful machine. I remember it vividly. It was a TGB Laser. Doesn't the name just seem to strike fear in you? It had a powerful 150cc engine. Its max speed topped the chart at 70 miles per hour. It was one bad machine. It even had a sporty paint job too. Its body was jet black with orange tiger stripes down the side. It spitted ominous black smog from its rear tailpipe. Yeah, I was the man. I was a Hell's Angel on a scooter with my matching helmet.

I spent over $3,000 dollars for that scooter and I enjoyed it for about two months. Then all of a sudden the wind blowing through my hair was less exciting. As winter set in, it sucked riding that thing in the rain. In the summer I sweated profusely at red lights. It was no longer fun to ride anymore.

As days passed the scooter sat idle in the garage more and more often. It started to develop a fine coat of dust. As more time passed I noticed work gloves hanging from the handle bars and boxes were perched comfortably where I once sat. The scooter became an extension of my shelves. I looked in amazement at my $3,000 shelf and noticed the plastic shelving system I brought from Wal-Mart for $50 was much more efficient. I shook my head sadly and thought of the money lost and went back inside to watch some TV.

This is a shining example of not controlling desire. I desired a scooter one day, so on impulse I went and brought one. Sure I thought about it for a little bit but I did not think about it nearly enough. I didn't analyze the purchase. I never considered the summer heat and how uncomfortable it would be in safety gear at red lights. I never consider the powerful Oklahoma winds that never seemed to cease. I never considered what I would do when the rainy season started.

After a couple of years of sitting idle I sold my scooter once I moved to Texas. I let it go for a pitiful sum too. I paid $3,000 and sold it for a pathetic $300. How can one get rich under these circumstances?

The ability to exercise self-control and conquer desire is paramount if one expects to become financially independent. If you cannot control yourself, there is nothing I can teach you to better your situation. If you don't have self-control, I suggest you try repeating this simple phrase. It is from "Invictus", a poem written by the English poet William Ernest Henley. "I am the master of my fate; the captain of my soul."

You can control your desires if you really want to. You can control yourself if you really want to. No one else will do it for you.

By repeating that simple phrase from Invictus, I'm introducing you to the power of suggestion. Suggestion is a process of inducing a thought in your mind and it is an extremely potent force. Throughout history people have exploited the power of suggestion to accomplish many great and wonderful things.

The mind is a curious entity. It is easily manipulated for better or for worst. As a kid I grew up with many children from broken homes. Their parents would call them names like stupid or regularly tell them they'd never be anything in life and through the power of suggestion, that's exactly what happened.

I hear two of my close childhood friends went to jail for murder and my other friends are all leading lackluster lives. These were creative kids too with so much potential but through suggestion, they started to believe they were incapable. They started to believe they couldn't prosper. So they didn't.

Use suggestion for your own benefit. Leverage its power. Manipulate it and use it to your own advantage. You'll come to believe in yourself and once you believe in yourself; there are no limitations. Everything and anything is possible.

Chapter 3

Whatever your hand finds to do, do it with all your might.

-Ecclesiastes 9:10

Minimum Wage and America's economic reality

The simple fact is there are more minimum wage earners than high income earners. Blue collar workers significantly outnumber white collar professionals. America is a minimum wage society. Let's shift gears for a second and examine why we have a federal minimum wage.

In the early 1900s the industrial age was in full effect. America's production was unequalled in the free world as factories spewed out an array of products from automobiles to textiles. Along with the rise of the industrial era came the rise of sweatshops.

Sweatshops proliferated in the early 1900s. Out of the ashes of the Civil War rose factories eager to employ children and women to dangerous labor at substandard wages. I consider it a mini dark age for capitalism. American industries sacrificed values and morals for profits. It was an unholy era. At one point the federal government motivated by advocacy groups stepped in and fixed this madness by setting a minimum wage.

The federal minimum wage is the minimum amount a worker can be paid for labor. To pay an employee less is in most cases illegal. At the time of this writing the federal minimum wage is $7.25 per hour, effective July 24, 2009. If you are being paid less than this I think you need to call someone in the United States Department of Labor immediately because you are getting hosed and probably have been for some time. Tipped employees like waiters and waitresses are treated differently.

Some economists argue that increasing minimum wage decreases jobs. Their argument is by increasing minimum wage companies will be more selective in how they hire. They will hire workers with a greater skill set commensurate to the pay. The least skilled workers will be effectively priced out of the market.

I believe we probably need to be careful in how we treat minimum wage but I am not convinced we should let the market set wages. I'd rather have fewer jobs and accept some unemployment than have zero unemployment with sweatshops everywhere. Corporate America has proven time and time again that values come in second to greed so I'm glad minimum wage is here to stay but we need to handle it carefully.

If workers demand more money companies simply pass the price of increased wages off on consumers. These are usually the very workers demanding higher wages! Besides people need to understand it is not about how much you make. It is about what you do with what you earn. If you give people more money, they simply spend more. It doesn't solve the problem.

I know what many of you are thinking. Can you really get rich off of minimum wage? I think you can. If fact I know you can and in the following chapters, I'll show you how.

Every day I encounter minimum wage workers. I see them in the sandwich shops. I see them in retail stores. I see them at hamburger stands. Most of my extended family earns minimum wage, struggling to pay the rent and put food on the table but I'm here to say they don't have to.

America has always been the land of opportunity. It has always been the land of plenty and there is plenty for everyone! You just need to control yourself and know how to make your money grow. And grow it will just like flowers in a garden or a weed that seems to appear out of nowhere on your freshly mowed lawn. You just have to have an open mind and listen to what I have to say.

Economist will continue to debate minimum wage forever. Some argue for it; others against it. I'm just glad that it's here to stay but remember having a minimum wage has done very little to reduce poverty levels. Poverty is more connected to our actions and how we think rather than some minimum pay for labor.

Chapter 4

Most of the world's useful work is done by people who are pressed for time, or are tired, or don't feel well.

-Douglas Freeman

Work, Labor and Exerting Energy

Many people ask me how to get rich without working. I'm here to tell you it is simply not possible. You must labor to get rich. Your ability to accumulate wealth is not tied to your income but it is directly proportional to your labor. Your labor brings you earnings but here is the beauty of it; your earnings in turn can labor for you.

Money is way more efficient than you. It labors 24 hours a day, 365 days a year. It doesn't take vacations nor demand benefits. Money will never ask you for a pay raise. It will labor without question for you for generations.

The curious part is while money labors, it produces more money as it labors! Soon you'll have a mass of coins diligently working hard for you from sun up to sun down but you must start with your own labor to earn your initial investment.

Besides work is good for you, it's good for your body and your soul. Scripture comments on the value of work and so does other religions. The point is work is critical for holistic health. Work builds your self-confidence. Work makes one feel a valued member of society. A man who works is more likely to respect laws and take care of his spouse and his children. Work is vital to self-esteem.

I've been exposed to some people who haven't earned an honest day's living in their lives and they are a depressing lot. They always whine about what they don't have and blame others for their situation. They are full of excuses and shy away from personal responsibility. These are the people hardest to reach. They continually look for someone to help them instead of them helping themselves.

These are the very people who will benefit the most from steady employment but their self-confidence is so low they are more content to waste away never challenging themselves, never tasting failure and experiencing rejection. These people are safe and secure in poverty. This book will not help these people.

But for those currently earning and for those who intend to earn in the near future, this book is for you. After you read this one I want you to buy a book called "The Richest Man in Babylon" by George S. Clason. In his book he says "wealth grows wherever men exert energy" and this is the absolute truth.

Let me give you an example. I'll use my neighborhood. It is a middle-class neighborhood with new homes popping up everywhere. Currently we are in the last phase of the development project. For every home under construction there are empty lots sitting next to it. Suppose, in my division, there are three empty lots. Let's say the lots are arranged with one lot in the middle and a lot on both sides to it. Suppose the man who owns the middle lot decides to build a house on it. The man pays a contractor to lay the foundation. He goes on to hire and pay framers next. Then he pays a contractor to place plywood over the frame. He goes on and on paying out cash for this and that until the house is finished. But is he poorer? No. The house is worth just as much as he spent on it and maybe more and he's made many men richer. The foundation guy has a part of it. The framers have some and so on. Just having a house on his lot increases the value of the other two lots next to it. So he's made his neighbors richer too. Wealth grows wherever there is labor and it grows in magic and mysterious ways. I truly believe wealth is unlimited.

Real estate developers often take barren, useless land and turn it into something special. Has anyone heard of a place called Las Vegas? Las Vegas is located in a valley desert. Undeveloped it was an awful looking place, devoid of flowers and grass. Water has to be piped in from other places because it's basically a desert wasteland but Las Vegas is a shining example of how labor can produce wealth without limits. One can take barren land and create an oasis through labor!

Let's consider Victorville, California. It is located on the southwest edge of the Mojave Desert about 81 miles northeast of Los Angeles. Annual rainfall is just over 6 inches. In short it is a dry and scorching place. I suppose if there is a hell on earth, Victorville, California is it. Victorville has not only survived, it has thrived! According to Sperling's BestPlaces, Victorville has a future job growth of over 10% and this city is located in the most inhospitable place. Victorville is another example of wherever labor is exerted, wealth grows.

By now you're growing impatient. I can feel it. You are wondering where and when the real education starts. You want to know how to get rich off a minimum wage income. We'll get to that and we'll get to it soon but first we have to visit a boring but critically important topic. It's called accounting.

Chapter 5

Every man, however intelligent, needs the advice of some wise friend in the affairs of life.

-Plautus

Personal Accounting

I'm not going to turn you into a certified accountant. I don't have the time or the energy for that and you probably don't want to sit through that painful experience either. What I will do for you is show you applicable accounting principles that are meaningful to real life.

That part is important to me. In school you are taught so many things. A lot of it isn't useful in your everyday life. In college I studied algebraic equations and trigonometry. Although a few concepts have been helpful the majority of it was a waste of time. Don't get me wrong I want you to stay in school because it is important but I really want you to know the real learning starts after you leave the classroom.

Schools continue to do well at teaching the three Rs, reading, writing and arithmetic but they steadily continue to fail to produce adults with basic life skills like shared human values and morals. You'll never really succeed in life without these. You must have a good understanding of right and wrong. Additionally you will never succeed without relationship skills. We need to know how to treat another person and interact with others otherwise all of your relationships will likely fail. Science can help with this too. We just have to go out and seek the information since it is not in schools.

Lastly we need personal financial management skills. We need to know how to budget and live within our means. After we have that crucial skill down then we need to know how to track our expenditures and understand our CASH FLOW.

Investopedia.com, one of my favorite websites, defines cash flow as "A revenue or expense stream that changes a cash account over a given period." I've seen it defined in other ways but I really like this definition because it tracks money in and out.

You must track and understand your cash flow if you intend to be relatively rich. The poor, working class, middle class and wealthy all have distinct cash flow. The poor may have income coming in but it rarely covers their expenses. I consider poor people the folks languishing on government assistance. They are not only poor financially but they are poor in their minds. They usually lack self-confidence and ambition and this is a travesty because I know so many of them have so much potential.

The working class cash flow is similar to the poor. The difference is they have more income coming in. These are your folks with actual jobs. They get up in the mornings and contribute to society and are rewarded with a paycheck. These are the people that will benefit most from this book. These are the people I wrote this book for. Now the working class cash flow follows the same pattern as the poor. They have income coming in and they consume all of it monthly on expenses. It doesn't have to be like that but it usually is the case.

The middle class cash flow is similar to the working class with an exception. The middle class may have some perceived assets. This normally takes the shape of the home they live in. With pride they'll post pictures of their home on Facebook and email photos of it to their high school friends but the reality is that home is probably sucking them dry. They are spending loads of money on mortgage payments, property taxes, home maintenance and utilities and so on. The hemorrhaging of money doesn't stop when you own a home. So I challenge all conventional thinking of a home being a great investment. It may be an investment but not a great one. There are plenty of places you can put money that will grow faster, safer and with greater liquidity.

The last group is the wealthy; the wealthy focus on income. Nothing else matters it's that simple. That's why understanding cash flow is so important. In order to be wealthy you need to know how much income you have coming in and where it is going. You need to know how much you have left after all your expenses are paid. Tracking and understanding cash flow is the real key to wealth. If there is any concept you must understand; you must understand cash flow. Cash flow is the only key to wealth. A wallet will quickly empty so will a purse unless there is a steady stream of income nourishing it. The wealthy are experts at managing and understanding cash flow. They have more income coming in then they spend and mastering cash flow in this manner is a CHOICE! You must choose to monitor and track your expenses. You must choose to spend less than you earn. You must choose to save and invest. The wealthy choose to spend less than their incomes. The wealthy reject a negative cash flow and choose a keep their cash flow positive. This is a choice you must make in order to become financially independent and thrive. If not you will struggle for the scraps of society all your life. The choice is yours.

Let's look at a sample depicting cash flow. Alright I'll be honest. It was mine at some point in my life.

Monthly Cash flow

Mortgage:	($926)
Internet:	($55)
Cell phones:	($100)
Netflix	($10)
Auto Insurance	($26)
Satellite TV	($45)
Utilities: electric, water, trash	($200)
Property taxes:	($91)
Food:	($400)
Alimony:	($500)
Child support:	($325)
Gas	($125)
Allowances:	($40)
Income from stocks	$11
Income from salary	$6,300
Income from real estate	$330
Total positive cash flow	$3,799

Let's look this depressing thing over. I see a hefty mortgage payment, lovely property taxes, child support and alimony as well as other expenses. But wait! There is a bright side! There is income from a rental property, income from stock dividends and a salary! Yay for a salary! Working is the only way to go. Working gives one existence meaning but back to the lesson at hand. This is the level of detail we need to track our cash flow and we ALWAYS want to keep our cash flow positive. A negative cash flow is NOT good. It means you are in the black and trouble is on the way. A positive cash flow is fantastic. A positive cash flow means you'll have money to invest to grow your assets. Purchasing and holding assets is vital. Assets permit money to work hard for you instead of you working hard for money but what exactly is an asset?

Chapter 6

Without a plan we keep covering old territory.

-Rick Pitino

Assets and Liabilities

Many people think they have assets all figured out. I'm here to say they have it wrong. Even a lot of the so-called financial experts have the definition of an asset wrong. Out of all the definitions out there, I prefer the one used by Mr. Robert Kiyosaki in his book "Rich Dad, Poor Dad." In his book he called an asset "anything that puts money in your pocket." I think this description is brilliant. It is brilliant in its simplicity. It is brilliant in its purpose and it is a direct challenge to traditional lines of thought.

Many people believe all stocks, bonds and real estate are assets. I do not believe this. I argue the only way these entities are assets is if they put money in your pocket after you purchase them. Using this line of thought this excludes the majority of small-capitalization stocks. Why? It is quite simply this. The stocks don't put money in your pockets. Small-caps could go broke tomorrow and your principal is lost. Dividend stocks can go bankrupt too but the risk is mitigated by the steady stream of income they pay.

If you recall income is the true path to wealth. With income you can conquer your cash flow. You should strive for the point in time where your income generated by your assets surpasses your expenses. Small capitalization stocks don't generate income and therefore cannot assist you in this worthy endeavor. With that said I argue one should reject all small capitalization stocks that do not pay dividends.

This is in huge conflict with what many economists, stock brokers, fund managers, corporations and probably your friends and relatives believe. Some look at small capitalization stocks and mutual funds as a critical element to long-term wealth. I feel these approaches increase risk. I think someone with a high allocation of small caps is trying to gain wealth too fast and I believe rapid wealth is a fool's errand. Real, meaningful wealth should come slowly. Those who gain wealth quickly seem to lose it just as fast. Consider those you know who recently received an inheritance. How about lottery winners? Their wealth probably disappeared in a short time. The only meaningful wealth is acquired slowly and comes through definite purpose and wisdom.

I think a better way to real wealth is to mitigate risk and loss of your principal. Money is hard-earned and one must carefully evaluate investments and employ it with caution to reduce prospects of loss. Loss is the enemy and the greatest danger to our long-term financial health. Stay away from any stock, bond, mutual fund or a real estate purchase that doesn't put money in your pocket. Anything else is NOT an asset because no money is returned to you. With that said let's look at the most common misconception of an asset, a house.

People save all their lives for their own home. They store cash for years to buy the biggest money drain of all time, a house. Let me ask you this. How is your home an asset? How much money does it add to your checking account? Everyone across the board will say zero unless you are renting out rooms or something like that. I'm guessing for 99% of Americans a home is not an asset.

Owning your own home makes you poorer and slows down your progress towards true financial independence. Let's explore this non-traditional line of thought. By owning your own home you incur dreaded property taxes. In some communities real estate taxation is ridiculous too. For example I pay a monthly mortgage payment of $926 and $333.17 of that payment goes to local property taxes. If my knowledge of mathematics doesn't fail me 36% of my mortgage payment goes to taxes. Unbelievable! Let's continue exploring a home as an asset.

A home steadily drains you of your hard earned money. With home ownership comes home maintenance. There are leaky pipes and clogged drains. There are landscaping costs. That annual fertilizer for your plush green lawn isn't free. It comes with a cost. What about pest control? That's another necessary expense. There is sprinkler maintenance, roof repair, safety upgrades and rotted fascia. There are exposed beams in the foundation, nesting materials in the attic, squeaky doors, poor chalking and inoperable ceiling fans. These expenses are why I reject the concept of owning your own home with a mortgage.

If you rented, your housing costs are fixed. Usually you aren't required to mow the yard or repair that leaky faucet. Your landlord is responsible for that. If you reject homeownership your surplus cash can go to purchasing real income producing assets rather than supporting your greatest liability, your home.

Some will argue against my line of thought and point out the equity you build in a home. A home normally increases a paltry 5% in value in most areas in the absence of some weird housing bubble like the one we experienced in the mid to late 2000s. Given this rate of return you'd do much better moving your surplus cash into stocks and mutual funds instead. There you are looking at an average of 8% to 10% in annual returns and this small difference adds up significantly over time. Let's demonstrate with real numbers.

Suppose you had some excess cash and you purchased a home for $100,000. With our reasonable assumption of a 5% annual increase in value, your home would be worth $164,700.95 in 10 years. In reality this wouldn't be your net return. Throughout that decade you would have been spending to upkeep your home. You would have spent on repainting, repair, weed killer, WD-40 and so on but let's suppose you put the money in stocks instead.

Suppose you placed the money in a low-risk mutual fund. Suppose it returned about 8% annually. Over that same decade you would have amassed $221,964.02. What's your net return? It is $221.964.02 minus any income taxes. There were no leaky faucets slicing into your return. There wasn't any repainting or property taxes. There wasn't anything out of your pocket. If I only would have known back then what I know now; I'd probably be a multi-millionaire. Stay away from a mortgage. If you can't buy a home with cash don't buy one. It's not in your best financial interests. I do recognize there is a cultural reason that drives you to want to purchase your own home and I'll help you satisfy that need if you are compelled to do so.

If you must own your own home for your own sanity; you should purchase a very modest one to reduce potential conflict with your goal of financial independence. You should purchase a home that gives you just enough space. This will keep your utilities down and lower your property taxes. You should consider working class neighborhoods opposed to apparent affluent one. I say apparent because many of these families are one paycheck away from being homeless.

If you do purchase your own home, for your financial independence, you should consider it a life-long commitment. Transaction costs for real-estate are expensive. Realtors get rich off the guys who purchase and sell homes in short periods. If you buy a home expect to keep it for life, for better or for worse. If you move expect to rent it out. Due to this commitment this is precisely why you must carefully consider how much home you can afford.

Here is probably another challenge to traditional thinking. Bonds are a fantastic asset! Why? Bonds continually pay you monthly or sometimes quarterly. They fit the very definition of an asset. Bonds put money in your pocket. They don't take any of it out. Some of you may be thinking bonds are silly investments with pathetic rates of return.

I agree some bonds have rates of returns so small; they are ridiculous to own but some don't. Some bonds return unbelievable rates. The investment company Vanguard has a few high-yield corporate bond funds that return over 8% annually but these high returns don't come without a price. These bonds are usually B-rated bonds commonly called junk bonds. They carry significantly more risk because these are usually corporations that are just getting started or established businesses having credit difficulties. Some of these bonds will default but you can reduce your risk by investing in a corporate bond fund. I'm 99.9% sure your whole portfolio of junk bonds won't fail. Let's look at some numbers.

At the time of this writing **Vanguard's High-Yield Corporate fund** has an annual rate of return of 8.88% since the fund's inception. Let's suppose you invested $20,000 over time in this fund. At an average rate of 8.88% you'd realize an additional $1,760 in annual income without you lifting a finger. This turns out to be approximately $146.66 a month.

Let's say you really dig this concept and you're able to sock away $100,000. At an average rate of 8.88% you'd realize an additional $8,800 in annual income. That's more than some people make all year and you'd make that without lifting a finger or working a second job. This turns out to be an extra $733.33 monthly. This target is well in the grasp of the average American. This target is well in the grasp of someone working minimum wage and it could turn out to be a nifty supplemental income. Remember at some point you may not be able to work.

The human body is a magical entity but no one as of yet can fully halt the aging process. Everyone's body eventually breaks down no matter how healthy you eat or how regularly you exercise. It is a natural fact of life therefore you should prepare yourself for that inevitability. There are other reasons to buy assets that put money in your pocket and shun liabilities like a home.

You may become unemployed at some point. Many Americans experience a job loss or change at some point in their lives. At the time of this writing the unemployment rate is a hefty 10%. Plenty of people are presently out of work. Wouldn't it nice if they had some real income from assets they could tap into? Think of all the stress this would relieve them from. Unemployment insurance is temporary. Those benefits normally run out in six months or a year in some special cases but with income producing assets in your portfolio you'd have a steady stream of income to help you through the tough times.

You are now armed with crucial information about assets and liabilities. By now you should understand the difference. You now know to buy assets and run from liabilities. Next we are going to get into budgeting. Without budgeting financial security and wealth accumulation isn't possible. Budgeting is the key to finding surplus capital we can use to grow our portfolio and establish our financial empire.

Chapter 7

He who conquers others is strong; He who conquers himself is mighty.

-Lao Tzu

Budgeting

Perhaps nothing makes a person cringe more than hearing the word budget. Some of us don't even know what the word means. I argue most Americans are familiar with the word but rarely practice it. If your finances are out of control it is not your fault. If it isn't your fault; whose fault is it?

Don't get me wrong I totally believe in personal responsibility but no one has taught you how to budget. The public schools have failed miserably in this area.

They teach reading, writing and arithmetic but nothing else.

I'm not writing this book to beat up our educational system. Schools are overcrowded, under-funded and teachers are overworked but if teaching budgeting isn't our educational system's responsibility then whose responsibility is it? Is it the government's responsibility?

Ah yes. As people we always expect the government to solve our individual shortcomings. If we do not save for old age, no problem, the government will take care of us. If we choose not to work, no problem, the government is there with welfare. If we choose not to go to school but we need more money, no problem, the government will redistribute wealth. Historically government is the problem rather than a solution.

Consider this; people have existed over five thousand years. We lived and endured that entire time without taxes, welfare and social security. These three social entities were inventions concocted in the early 1900s around the time of the Great Depression and I believe these programs have created more harm than good.

By giving handouts the government has unintentionally created an environment of dependency. The government has unintentionally robbed entire segments of its population of their self-esteem.

Here's a life lesson, when you give someone something for free. They will never, ever appreciate it. They may smile in your face at the time but the reality is if they don't work and earn it with their own sweat, blood and tears; they'll take it for granted. The take it for granted attitude is running amuck in the lower economic neighborhoods all across America. Instead of being thankful they continue to demand more handouts.

The lower economic classes continue to take gifts from America's taxpayers for granted. You give them welfare for free; next they demand free healthcare. You give them healthcare for free; next they demand free housing and the list goes on and on. If you want to fix poverty you must first fix the poor's thinking. If you fix their thinking you fix their self-esteem. If you fix their self-esteem, they can reach their full potential, grow and prosper. I've said it before and I'll say it again, every human is loaded with God given potential. If only we would harness it.

No. It is not the government's responsibility to teach us budgeting. The government would probably jack it up anyway if given the chance. It is up to us to teach ourselves but how do you teach yourself something you don't even know? This is where everyone divides after high school. For some people education ends after high school while others seek to continually learn new things that they don't know. It is the latter that go on to do great and meaningful things in life. As for me I discovered budgeting by accident while seeking knowledge.

In 2009 a divorce set me back financially. I had to liquidate a lot of my assets as part of the settlement. I was also ordered to pay spousal support for three years. This put a serious strain on my finances. Overall about $60,000 in losses is attributed to my divorce but it was well-worth it. I received primary custody of my two kids and I refused child support from my ex when the judge offered it. Overall it was a bargain and I'd do it a million times over if given the chance.

The initial lump sum payment and the regular spousal support threatened my lifestyle. I really only had one option I had to reduce my standard of living. I had bitter days following the divorce. My confidence and self-esteem fell. I started spending to feel better. I was going nowhere fast. In a desperate attempt to recapture what was lost I went to the local bookstore for some self-help audio-books. Besides the "Power of Positive Thinking" by Dr. Norman Vincent Peale I picked up "The Richest Man in Babylon" by George S. Clason.

These are two very different books but these books helped me out of my rut and started me towards meaningful change. The "Power of Positive Thinking" corrected my mind. "The Richest Man in Babylon" shaped my budgeting and financial philosophy. Using "The Richest Man in Babylon" I developed my own budgeting philosophy to gain financial independence. I call it the 85% method.

The 85% method is a way of life. It is quite simply this. You live on 85% of your net-income. This gives you a 15% surplus. For now do not stress about that surplus. We'll put it to good use soon in future chapters. For now focus on the 85% method.

If you recall from previous chapters we talked about your monthly cash flow. We talked about how important it was to track it accurately. Do you see why now? By listing our itemized cash flow we can reduce or eliminate expenses to get us within the 85% range.

Perhaps you're spending $125 monthly on a cable TV, digital phone and internet. What if another company offered a bundle of equal quality for just $90? What if you're overspending on groceries? Maybe you should refrain from those pre-package, prepared, overpriced, fried jalapeno poppers. Do you recall our discussion about choices? It is all about what you choose for yourself. Will you choose to live from paycheck to paycheck or will you choose financial independence?

You must choose the 85% method for financial freedom. Look hard at your expenditures and reduce and eliminate any waste. Creatively seek to drop your expenses even further until you are within the 85% range. This may mean choosing a store brand cereal like Wal-Mart's "Great Value" over Kellogg. The cost difference is substantial yet the taste and nutritional value is practically the same.

It is important to note the 85% method includes everything. It includes your housing costs, utilities, food, gas, auto maintenance, cell phone, cable TV, insurance, entertainment expenditures and internet. The 85% must include your entire cost of living. If something is pushing you over the 85% mark you need to eliminate it or drop something else of lesser value to you out of your budget. It is paramount to live under your means! If you do not live under your means I CANNOT teach you and you will NEVER become financially independent!

Housing expenses normally push people over the edge. People spend too much on a mortgage. People spend too much on rent. Listen to me and hear me loud and clear. Your housing costs should never be greater than 20% of your monthly income.

Now let's put all of this together in an example. Suppose you work part-time and bring home $1,100 monthly. If you listen to what I have to say 85% is targeted towards living expenses. That works out to $935. If you keep listening to me 20% is targeted towards your housing costs. This works out to $220. That leaves you $715 to cover all your other expenses and you still have a 15% surplus or $165 leftover for investment.

Now some of you in high cost areas may argue you can't find rent that cheap but I beg to differ because Section 8 runs unabated in high cost communities. With the federal government paying a sizable portion of your housing cost, you can still stay within the 20% range and put money away. If you have no access to Section 8 you should simply move to another area or state. America is loaded with communities where this type of rental cost isn't a dream. What about renting a room? There are all kinds of options. You need to have the desire and courage to pursue a better life.

Now I cannot complete this chapter without giving you ideas on where to store your 85% cost of living allowance. It must be in a respectable bank or credit union with low fees and is FDIC insured. FDIC stands for Federal Deposit Insurance Corporation. The FDIC is an independent agency created by Congress in 1933. The specific act was the Glass-Steagall Act.

Prior to the Glass-Steagall Act if a bank failed the depositors were simply out of luck. FDIC deposit insurance protects the money in your account up to $250,000 per depositor. FDIC was a significant victory for Congress. Its value and worth has stood for generations since its inception and it will stand for generations more. FDIC prevents a run on banks. A run on banks is a condition where depositors believe a bank's failure is imminent and rush to withdraw their funds. The banks are obligated to comply. Fueled by emotion, depositor after depositor withdraws their money forcing the institution to fail. Why? I'll answer that question with a "what if" scenario. What if every depositor went to the bank at the same time and withdrew their money? The result is the bank instantly goes bankrupt barring outside intervention because not all of the money is there at one time.

"What? My money isn't there." You ask angrily.

Nope, it isn't. It has been loaned out. The guy driving that flashy car with the $800 monthly payment and sporty rims spent part of it. So did your neighbor down the street living in a mini-mansion. You know the guy paying a $3,000 monthly mortgage payment on a bus driver's salary. Banks loan our money to make more money. They simply take money from another account to pay you when you withdraw funds. This is the easiest way to understand how our banking system works. FDIC insurance is the bedrock that upholds the very framework of our entire financial system. It is one of the few programs politicians have gotten right.

So who should you bank with? Personally, I bank with USAA. It stands for United Services Automobile Association. In my humble opinion there is no better bank. In the past USAA only served military but things have changed. Now anyone can open checking and savings accounts with USAA. USAA has low fees and excellent customer service. If you decide to use USAA it is recommended you have internet access since it is largely a self-service bank. Self-service means you do most of your transactions yourself over the internet. You can transfer funds and pay your bills. You will have to use ATMs to get cash. USAA only has a few full service locations but they more than make up for this inconvenience with their low fees. USAA even includes free internet based budgeting software to help you track your spending too.

In the upcoming chapters we are going to walk you further down the road of financial independence by showing you what to do with that surplus 15%. I warn you it is a bumpy road. It will challenge your resolve, strength and determination but end of the road is very pleasant. You will be free from the daily stress of wondering where your next meal is coming from or that nagging question of "will I have enough to pay my utilities?" The 85% method is the truth. You just have to accept it as such and ready yourself for what comes next. Do you remember the surplus 15% we set aside? In the next chapter I'm going to show you what to do with 5% of that surplus.

Chapter 8

Opportunity follows struggle. It follows effort. It follows hard work. It doesn't come before.

-Shelby Steele

Emergency Fund

Before we get started on this topic I want to tell you a tale. It is a biblical story with tremendous applicability to life today. It is the story of Joseph. According to scripture Joseph was the 11th son of a guy named Israel and a woman named Rachael. According to the Bible out of all the children Israel loved his son Joseph the most.

Israel loved Joseph so much he brought him a fancy, colorful coat and gave it to him. Joseph liked the coat and proudly shown it to his brothers but his brothers were straight pissed! They wanted a coat too! Heck it was chilly and there was no central heat at the time so I guess I understand.

The purchase of the new coat and a couple of dreams Joseph had were the final straws that broke the camel's back. Joseph's brothers plotted his murder but murdering their brother was harder than they thought so instead of killing the dude; they sold him into slavery. After Joseph was sold into slavery the evil crew of brothers rushed back and told their dad Joseph was killed by a wild beast. They brought Joseph's fancy coat splattered with goat's blood back as proof. To say Israel was bummed at the news is an understatement.

Now Joseph was brought to Egypt as a slave. He was sold to a guy named Potiphar, the captain of the Pharaoh's guard. Here Joseph excelled. He was quickly promoted to oversee the Potiphar's entire household. His potential was unlimited but despair and setbacks lurked around the corner.

Potiphar's wife fancied Joseph but he refused her advances. When she grew tired of this rejection; she concocted a false story of an attempted sexual assault and Joseph was promptly arrested and imprisoned.

In prison Joseph befriended the royal cup bearer who found himself in prison after offending the king. It seems everyone found themselves in prison in those days huh? One day the cup bearer had a dream and asked Joseph what the dream meant.

Joseph interpreted the dream to mean the cup bearer would be reinstated in three days. As the story goes three days later the cup bearer was found innocent and reinstated just as predicted.

Two years passed. One day the Pharaoh had two dreams that deeply disturbed him. He dreamt of seven lean cows which rose out of the river and devoured seven fat cows. Additionally he dreamt of seven withered ears of grain which devoured seven fat ears. He summoned his wise men to interpret the dreams but they were unsuccessful. This troubled Pharaoh even further.

At this time the cup bearer remembered Joseph and his incredible knack for interpreting dreams and retold his own story to Pharaoh.

Pharaoh was intrigued and ordered Joseph be brought before him. In Joseph's presence Pharaoh retold his dreams. Upon conclusion of his tale he stared at Joseph awaiting the dream's interpretation. Joseph didn't disappoint either. Without hesitation he concluded the dreams meant Egypt would experience seven years of plenty followed by seven years of famine and he advised Pharaoh to store surplus grain during the abundant years.

Pharaoh was impressed by Joseph's wisdom and ordered him permanently released from prison. On top of that he put Joseph in charge over all of Egypt, not bad for a former convict. To summarize the remaining events Joseph's prophecy was correct and events unfolded as he predicted. Joseph's reputation grew and so did his further successes.

I have one question for you. What is the moral of this story? Can you see it? The moral is simply this. In times of plenty you must prep yourself for the bad. This is why you need an emergency fund and this is what you should do with 5% of earnings.

Let's pretend your income is the grain and take 5% of your surplus and store it for hard times. I guarantee those hard times will come too. Maybe your car will break down or perhaps your washer will give out. Maybe Johnny's sneakers will prematurely age. You never know what life will throw at you. Your best option is to expect the unexpected and build an emergency fund.

Let's think of your emergency fund as a massive granite wall. It protects your long-term savings from threats and just as stonewalls secured towns and cities in early history, your emergency fund will secure you in modern times. It'll protect you from unexpected job loss and mayhem and all those events that seem to show their ugly heads at the most inopportune time.

Let's stick with our example and run some numbers. Suppose you net $1100 monthly. You budget 85% toward cost of living expenses. That works out to $935. Next you budget 5% of your net income towards an emergency fund. This works out to $55.

When you first start your emergency fund it won't appear to be capable of handling any emergencies but stay the course and revisit it in a few months. Then look at it after a year has past. In three months you'll have $165. After one year you'll have $660. The question I always get is how big should an emergency fund be?

Most experts will say three to six months of your net pay. So if you net $1100 monthly anywhere from $3300 to $6600. I disagree with this. I believe your EXPENSES should dictate the size of your emergency fund. For example let's look at the cash flow of a person working part-time making a working class salary.

Monthly Cash flow

Rent	($220)
Internet/phone:	($50)
Cell phones:	($49)
Netflix	($10)
Auto Insurance	($27)
Utilities: electric, water, trash	($150)
Food:	($150)
Life insurance	($50)
Emergency fund (5%)	($55)
Gas	($50)
Long-term Saving (10%)	($110)
Income from salary	$1,100

In this case not considering payments to the emergency fund and long term savings this individual's monthly expenses total $756. It is this amount, your total monthly EXPENSES that should drive the size of your emergency fund. Additionally I firmly believe your emergency fund should equal your monthly expenses times six. Sticking with this example this person's emergency fund should be $4536. Why so much?

By storing six months expenses you effectively secure yourself against unexpected job loss. Murphy's Law states "Anything that can go wrong will go wrong." We are in an era of outrageous deficits and out-of-control federal and state debts. Since federal and state politicians choose to avoid these touchy issues you can expect intense pressure on social programs like unemployment insurance when we reach the breaking point. It is better to prepare yourself than depend on the government.

I hope you've accepted the case for an emergency fund. Now let's talk about where to put it. A fantastic place for an emergency fund is a regular, old saving account. Sure there are other places you can put this cash for a slightly and I mean slightly higher interest rate but the important point is liquidity. If Murphy's Law proves accurate you will need those funds at some point and it is important that you can access the money quickly. Certificates of Deposits have nice rates but you are penalized severely for early withdrawals. Stay away from these types of accounts for your emergency fund. I recommend a regular saving account for your stash.

Some banks and credit unions offer a high-yield savings account if your account reaches a certain balance. You need to research this because the accounts are normally given a higher interest rate at no additional cost. The catch is you have to surpass the monetary threshold and ask for the special rate. Most of the time a bank or credit union won't voluntarily pay you more money unless you back them into a corner and ask.

Some mutual fund companies offer money market accounts. Money market accounts invest in government or corporate securities. Securities are financial entities such as banknotes or bonds. Money market accounts are excellent places to put your emergency fund. These accounts usually draw a higher rate of interest and are very liquid should you need the money. The only drawback is it usually takes several days for a transaction to clear if you sell your money market shares. With a regular saving account you'll have instant gratification and immediate access to your money should the need arise.

Chapter 9

To be upset over what you don't have is to waste what you do have.

-Ken Keyes, Jr.

Long-term Saving

The question on everyone's mind is what is this long-term saving stuff about? Some want to know why we even need to save for the future. Won't Social Security provide for us when we get old?

Social Security was never really designed to supply all of a person's needs when they are no longer able to work. It was only designed as a supplement. Social security was signed into law in 1935 by President Franklin D. Roosevelt. It was part of Roosevelt's New Deal initiative. The New Deal was the driving mechanism that emerged America from the Great Depression.

To sum it all up Americans were tired. Americans were tired of the elderly living in poverty. They were tired of the aged and disabled going hungry. Americans called for moral responsibility, action and protection of our most vulnerable citizens and President Roosevelt delivered. What he didn't know at that time is the potential pitfalls of this entitlement program. He had no idea he opened Pandora's Box.

Social Security is funded by dedicated payroll taxes called Federal Insurance Contributions Act (FICA). It is dependent on current workers funding Social Security checks of those who can't. Look at it like an allowance. Instead of your elderly dad giving you an allowance you are giving him one providing you are working, earning an income and paying taxes.

This system is fine as long as you have more workers than elderly drawing benefits. Here lies the problem. After World War II Americans came back from the Great War and made babies, lots of babies. There was a significant population explosion as Americans felt great about life and the future. However as time has passed Americans have abandoned larger families in favor of smaller ones. We know now children cost a lot of money and we want more money to do things and enjoy life. Over time our families have gotten smaller and smaller.

This has had an unexpected effect. Since we have smaller families, we have a smaller workforce. An imbalance has occurred. We have more elderly drawing Social Security benefits than workers paying into the system.

This is resulting in less than desirable effects. Since we don't have enough workers to fund benefits for the elderly; our government borrows money to fund the difference. It does this by issuing government bonds. Right now our friends in China are the largest foreign holder of American debt.

The United States Social Security program is the largest social program in the world resulting in 37% of government's expenditures. Unfortunately this program is getting out of control. Elderly people are living longer and drawing more benefits and we have an insufficient amount of workers. Add these two things together and you get a recipe for disaster.

The Social Security trust fund is well on its way to exhausting its entire store of capital and the politicians continue to do nothing. I think sweeping changes are coming soon.

The eligibility age to draw benefits will certainly rise in the near future. Projected benefits will certainly be cut. It is the only way since we've ignored our federal debt and overspent time and time again.

This is why long-term saving is so important. There is great potential our government will be incapable of providing us an income when we can no longer work. This puts the ball back in our court. It is the very definition of personal responsibility. This is why you must pay yourself first.

The phrase "Pay yourself first" is often attributed to George S. Clason. It is regularly quoted in the text of his best-selling classic "The Richest Man in Babylon." I cannot stress this term enough. Every working person should store not less than 10% of their net income monthly for their future and their children's future.

With the power of compounding this will result in a sizable nest egg over time. In 2008 I published my first article on the value of compounding. In that story I used an example that demonstrated the power of compounding. I took 10% of the basic pay of our lowest-ranking military member and I compounded it annually at 8% for 20 years. This is the way it worked out. Ten percent of the basic pay of our lowest ranking military member was about $130.14 at the time. After compounding it annually at 8% for 20 years a person would have a balance of $73,970. Just $31,200 of this amount was their money. The other $42,770 is compounded interest. This is the true power of compounding. Let's look at our case study of the minimum wage earner from earlier and behold the magic of compounding. Let's look at their cash flow sheet again.

Monthly Cash flow

Rent	($220)
Internet/phone:	($50)
Cell phones:	($49)
Netflix	($10)
Auto Insurance	($27)
Utilities: electric, water, trash	($150)
Food:	($150)
Life insurance	($50)
Emergency fund (5%)	($55)
Gas	($50)
Long-term Saving (10%)	($110)
Income from salary	$1,100

Ok. It appears 10% of their net income is $110 dollars. Let's compound that amount at 8% the historical average of the stock market since its inception. We'll compound this amount annually for 10, 20 and 40 years and see what we come up with.

Assuming we start with no principal, that means zero. In 10 years we'll have $20,652.04. Now let's do it again. This time we'll compound it over 20 years. In 20 years we'd have $65,238.26. Not bad off a minimum wage income, huh. Let's do the math once more this time over 40 years. In 40 years assuming an 8% annual return, a minimum wage earner placing just 10% of their income away would amass $369,310.97! This is a respectable fortune by anyone's account.

This is power of compounding! Its magic is available for one and all. You must harness its power for yourself; no one will do it for you. Through your own labor, discipline and resolve you can realize the American dream. I beg you not to get left behind. Take what America offers. There is more than enough wealth in this nation for all.

So now you're storing 10% of your income and you're anxious to find a place to put it. I've got just the place but first we need to do some self-reflection. We need to find out just what type of person you are. Are you a risk-taker? Do you love to walk the mean streets of Los Angeles at night? Or do you avoid risk wherever possible? Do you pass on bungee-jumping for a nice game of Monopoly? It is essential we know ourselves intimately before we start investing. If we misread our strengths and weaknesses it will cost us thousands of dollars and set us back years from reaching our financial goals.

Investing is about risk but not all risk is the same. There are different levels. Some investments have low risk. Others have moderate risk. Still others carry high risk.

What level you choose to accept is 100% up to you. If you accept high risk you potentially stand to make a great profit. If you accept a lower risk your profit will be smaller but there is less danger of losing your principal.

You have to know YOU before you invest. If the thought of high risk investments disrupts your sleeping patterns and give you acid reflux disease the potential returns are not worth it. Your sanity and health are more important than money but if you sleep comfortably investing in small companies on the brink of bankruptcy by all means go for it. It totally depends on you.

With that said I'm against undo risk. I feel get rich quick stocks and investments invite loss of my capital so I avoid them all together. I believe it is unwise to expect massive returns in a short amount of time. Investing in risky stocks isn't investing at all. It's gambling. You might as well go out and buy a load of lottery tickets with your hard earned cash. There is a certain gratification in getting rich slow through your own labor. I can't really explain the feeling but trust me it is gratifying.

I'll suggest places to put your 10% but I won't steer you towards super risky investments. It goes against my principals and I'll never sacrifice my principals to sell books or for any other purpose. If one does not have values, what does one have?

By now you know my definition of assets. They need to earn you money. **Therefore I do not recommend any**

stock, bond or anything else that does not pay out dividends regularly. This excludes a lot of small capitalization stocks. This excludes real estate such as undeveloped land. This excludes baseball cards and coins produced at the U.S. Mint. This excludes anything that doesn't send you a big, fat check monthly, quarterly or annually. I know I'm stirring the hornet's nest here because there are people who have made millions on small capitalization stocks that don't pay dividends.

This is true. People have made millions but I wonder if that money has brought them lasting value because of how it was accumulated. Investing in that manner is gambling even when you do your due diligence. For every one person that made a million that way there are probably hundreds, if not thousands of others who went broke. Investing in small capitalization stocks encourages undo risks. I reject that philosophy for lower income earners and I reject those who support and promote it. It is just too risky for most people.

Let's get back to where I'd put my 10%. If I'm severely risk adverse I'd put it in a good mutual fund but it is important to understand you can still lose money in a mutual fund. Mutual funds are not risk free. Mutual funds are a collective investment scheme where you pool your money with others. The pooled money is then used to purchase individual stocks or corporate bonds. If I didn't define corporate bonds earlier let me do so now in simple terms. Corporate bonds are kind of like a promissory note. Do you remember the promissory notes from the game of "Life" when you were a kid? It's the same concept, money is provided to the corporation and the corporation promises to repay it.

There is an excellent investment company called Vanguard that specializes in mutual fund investments. Here is my disclosure I invest with Vanguard myself. I own a significant amount of **Vanguard Real Estate Investment Trust Admiral Shares** (REIT). It should be no surprise then I'd recommend this fund. The ticker is VGSLX.

This fund invests in companies that purchase office buildings, hotels and other types of real estate. It is less-diversified because it invests only in real estate but it pays great dividends and has low management fees. This means you can stick with my strategy of minimizing risks and buying assets that pay you.

Another Vanguard fund I'd recommend is the **Vanguard Wellesley Income Fund.** This is a 40 year old fund, income-oriented, investing in a nice mix of dividend stocks, bonds and short-term cash reserves. It takes about $3,000 to open an account but you can make additional investments with a little as $100. **This is the fund I recommend for the minimum wage or low-income earner!** There is less volatility with this fund, less risk and greater potential for capital preservation.

The last fund that deserves some attention is the **Vanguard High-Yield Corporate Fund.** This fund invests primarily in medium and low quality corporate bonds. These are often referred to as junk bonds. These are unproven companies with lower credit ratings or sometimes companies that have credit problems. There is significantly greater risk with junk bonds and **I do not recommend this fund for low-income earners.** But with greater risk comes greater reward and the fund minimizes risk somewhat but investing in many, many junk bonds. The potential for all of these B-rated borrowers defaulting is likely remote.

I have one more thing to tell you about mutual funds. All mutual funds have operating costs. These costs are associated with record-keeping, advertising and things of that nature. Therefore you need to research what the operating costs are before you invest. Sometimes mutual fund companies call operating costs **EXPENSE RATIOS.** Whatever you call them you must be mindful of these expenses because they reduce your realized return. For example if your operating costs are 1% annually and the fund returns an average annual return (AAR) of 8%; your net return is actually 7%. This is different than what is usually advertised. The advertised AAR doesn't consider any costs or fees. You must avoid any loaded funds. A load is a charge for either purchasing or selling your shares. Vanguard is the uncrowned king of no-load funds. Vanguard doesn't charge you for purchasing or selling shares from your accounts. **That is why Vanguard is the only company I'd recommend for low-income or minimum wage earners.**

As with any investment, investors must evaluate these things on their own and determine if these funds suit their own investment style and risk tolerance. All investments carry the possibility of loss of capital and if anyone ever tells you they have a sure thing, run like hell. There is no such thing as a sure thing. Remember it isn't the smartest people that get ahead; it's the boldest. There is no reward without risk. File that statement away and do with it as you will.

I have riskier recommendations for your 10% surplus if you want. For the truly bold I recommend individual stocks that pay dividends. This recommendation fits the true definition of an asset because it pays you money. Most individual stocks pay it on a quarterly or annual basis. With stock investing better research is a must. So let's start with my short-cuts for analyzing stocks.

I believe you can analyze stocks like the pros by knowing key valuation measures. Valuation measures are figures or statistics I use to determine whether or not a stock is a good investment but before I teach you how to evaluate stocks I need to show you where to find the information you need.

I do all of my stock research on entirely free sources. Yahoo! Finance is my favorite. Yahoo! Finance, Google Finance and others can provide all the data we need. I'd experiment with all the free financial websites until you find one you like best but most of them are setup the same. Most sites have a little text box where you can type in your ticker. For example go to Yahoo! Finance and find the quote box and type in WMT and press enter. (I wanted to use graphics to help you navigate through Yahoo! Finance but they don't show up well in eBooks so you are on your own…..bummer.)

This will usually take you to a **SUMMARY** page. The key values I care about on this page are P/E or price to earnings ratio and the DIV & Yield. If the DIV & Yield is N/A avoid this stock. It means this stock won't pay you anything. Your only hope is that the stock goes up in value one day and you sell it for a profit. **Only buying stocks that pays dividends is my first rule.** The higher the dividend yields the better but be cautious of unusually high dividend yields. There is probably a reason why these stocks are so undervalued and I'd wager their dividend will be cut soon. Dividend yield cannot be used by itself. You must ensure you compare it to a stock's payout ratio to get the full picture. We'll cover payout ratio soon but for now let's look at price to earnings ratios.

Price to earnings ratio is the price paid for a stock relative to its earnings. In other words it is the price you pay for every dollar of earnings. For example Wal-Mart's current P/E at the time of this writing is 13.71. What does this mean? You pay $13.71 for every $1 Wal-Mart earns. I hope that makes sense to you because I can't think of any other way to explain it. An ideal P/E is $1 for $1. I've never seen a P/E like that but one can always dream. P/E is a good ratio because it helps you determine whether or not a stock is undervalued, cheap or on-sale, whatever you want to call it.

How do you know if a stock is on-sale? I do this by comparing its P/E to the industry average P/E. Most sites have a place where you can find industry averages. On Yahoo! Finance there is a link on the summary page. It's on the left hand side under **COMPANY** information. Click on the **Industry** hyperlink. Towards the bottom, you'll see another hyperlink labeled **Industry Summary**, click on it.

Somewhere on the right side you'll see a box labeled **INDUSTRY STATISTICS** after the page pops up. Here is where you'll find the information you need. If the industry average is higher than the P/E of the stock you are interested in, you likely have an undervalued stock. Let's stay with our example. Suppose Wal-Mart has a P/E is 13.71 and the industry average is 16.3. Then Wal-Mart is undervalued. At the time of this writing this is actually the case. Stock analysts are whooping and hollering about Wal-Mart losing market share to competitors like Target. Investors are buying into the hype and selling Wal-Mart's stock in droves. When they sell I try and buy when it is a good stock and Wal-Mart is a great company. To be a great investor you need to control fear and steer clear of hype. If you can master your emotions you'll find bargain stocks all the time. You'll find so many you'll wish you had more money to invest. There is always an investment opportunity on Wall Street. **Buying undervalued stocks is my second rule.**

At the time of this writing Wal-Mart is undervalued but is it a good investment? We need more information to see if it is. Our next stop is the **INCOME STATEMENT**. From the summary page most free financial websites will have a link to the income statement. On Yahoo! Finance it's on the left side towards the bottom of the summary page.

On an income statement we care out two things **REVENUE** and **OPERATING INCOME or LOSS**. Let's start with total revenue. In stock investing you want to invest your hard-earned money in growing companies. You measure a company's growth by evaluating revenue.

If the trend of revenue is growing you can assume it will continue. Newton's First Law states objects in motion will stay in motion unless a force acts to change the motion. I believe this works for corporations too. Corporations increasing revenue will likely continue to increase revenues unless something acts to stop them. Some may question this wisdom but I point to success stories like Coca Cola, Microsoft and Google. Pull their income statements and see for yourself. Sometimes factors such as economic climate may decrease revenues for a year or two but overall the trend is up. **Buying stocks with increasing revenue is my third rule.**

Let's look at operating income or loss now. Increasing revenue is meaningless if the corporation isn't making a profit. Revenues can go up and up but if you're spending more than your making it is a fool's errand. Just look at the federal government for example. Gross Domestic Product keeps rising and the economy keeps growing but we're still spending more than we earn and its catching up with us. Corporations are the same way. Heck, don't even look at corporations; look at yourself. What if you kept earning more and more every year but you spent more than you earned. Eventually your household would implode. It isn't a question of if but when. **A good corporation effectively managed will have positive operating income and that is my fourth rule.**

Next we're going to check out some key statistics. Most websites have a link to the figures we need. On Yahoo! Finance it's on the summary page labeled **KEY STATISTICS** somewhere on the left side under company information.

The key statistics will give us access to many important stats, ratios and indicators. In a nutshell you'll find most of the critical information you need to evaluate stocks there. It is my third stop after the summary and income statement. There are a lot of statistics on the key statistics page so I'll highlight the statistics I find most useful.

We'll start with trailing P/E. This is the P/E for the four most recently completed quarters. This helps us evaluate the value of a stock. It helps us figure out whether or not a stock is on-sale.

Profit margin is next. This is an indicator of whether or not a company is profitable. **A positive profit margin is my fifth rule.** I really like profit margins above 7% but I do recognize some businesses like large retail stores have greater operating costs. These companies have to manage massive supply chains and large workforces. Wal-Mart stores are open 24 hours a day, 365 days a year. Maintaining operating hours like that isn't easy or cheap. It takes a lot of money and that cuts into profits. Corporations won't have any problems with lower but positive profit margins if their management is good but how do you know if their management is good?

You can get an idea about a corporation's management by evaluating some simple statistics. The two I evaluate are management effectiveness **RETURN ON ASSETS** and **RETURN ON EQUITY**. The return on assets stat indicates how well a company's leadership manages the assets under their control. Are they running a company into the ground or are they growing it? If the return on assets is negative it's probably the first one but if it's positive management is proving they can grow the value of the assets under their control and this is not an easy feat. Creating increasing value requires wisdom and that is something some upper managers lack. If a company is run unwisely it will show in their management effectiveness numbers.

Return on equity is a similar statistic. It answers a critical question. Are managers capable of choosing the right investment platforms for their surplus cash? Let me ask you this. Would you want a manager taking surplus cash from your company and buying risky penny stocks with it? Some managers do this very thing and it shows in their awful return on equity numbers. Wise managers and wise people hate loss of principal. They refuse to chase impossible returns on trendy goods, products or services. The speculative investment is a crap shoot. **Positive percentages for management effectiveness numbers is my sixth rule.**

I must tell you I despise debt. I really hate it. The very thought of owing someone really bugs me but all debt is not the same. There is good debt and there is bad debt. Debt taken to buy assets is good debt provided you get it under favorable terms. Suppose you take out a loan at 4.75% to purchase an investment property for $48,500.

Suppose you are able to rent this property out for $600 a month. In this scenario your monthly mortgage payment would be $303.52 yet you net $296.48 monthly from the income the property produces. Is this good debt or bad debt? Let's say it together, "Good debt!"

Debt taken to buy luxuries or other things that don't provide income is bad debt. What are those things? I'd say a car would fit this definition. How about furniture and appliances like washers and dryers? Is this good or bad debt? Let's say it together, "Bad debt!" I really hate bad debt. My recommendation to you is to stay away from it. This is good advice for you and for corporations.

That's why I check a company's balance sheet. I want to compare their cash on-hand against their leverage. Leverage is just a fancy term for debt. This gives me an idea of how close a company is to defaulting on their loans and possible bankruptcy.

Let's suppose Wal-Mart has $10.62B in available cash and they carry $56.82B in debt. In this fictional example that's a lot of debt. But is it? We need to consider their business. Wal-Mart has large warehouses and tons of merchandise. You have to incur a lot of debt to support this type of business. In an ideal situation I like a 50-50 split of cash on-hand and debt but I don't rule out a stock solely on that threshold. With $10B of cash on-hand Wal-Mart can make its debt payments for a while with no problems. Suppose a company had $1M in cash on-hand

and carried $50M in debt. I'd run away from their stock as fast as my legs would carry me because this company may default soon. I want good companies that pay good dividends. I want those dividend paychecks to keep coming for years and I want to avoid undo risk. To get what I'm looking for I still need more information. I need to check a company's **PAYOUT RATIO**.

Payout ratio measures the amount of earnings paid out to shareholders. This is a critical statistic for dividend stock investors. It gives you insight on a company's ability to sustain current dividends and a hint of their potential for raising dividends in the future. Payout ratios must be used correctly and I'll tell you how I use this neat statistic.

A company's payout ratio is expressed as a percentage and it shows how much of the earnings are paid to shareholders. For example if a company paid out everything it brought in through sales; the payout ratio would be 100%. If a company paid out 1/10 of everything it brought in; its payout ratio would be 10%.

Let's say you are part owner of a hotdog stand. You are unfortunate enough to have to work the stand while the other partner sits at home eating chips and watching the ballgame. Let's say you sold 100 hotdogs at $1 each. You and your partner agreed to a payout ratio of 10%. With this example you need to pay your partner $10 for every $100 of revenue.

This is exactly how payout ratio works with large corporations. There are more shareholders and there is more money at stake but it is essentially the same. **For my seventh rule I invest in companies with payout ratios below 50%.** This gives me a good possibility dividends will grow over time.

Let's get back to our example. Suppose Wal-Mart's payout ratio is 29% percent. Throughout history Wal-Mart has demonstrated over time it isn't afraid to return money to shareholders. Wal-Mart has raised dividends annually since at least 1999 and I believe Wal-Mart will continue raising dividends in the future considering their track record. Wal-Mart is winning big time on our analysis but how do **INSIDERS** feel about the corporation.

Insiders are people who actually work for Wal-Mart. An insider can be that old lady behind the jewelry counter or the elderly guy greeting you at the door. An insider can be the big shots too. Insiders could be corporate executives privy to all the financial secrets of the business. That's why shares held by insiders are important. These folks are intimately familiar with the company. The associates are able to see how much consumer traffic goes in and out on a daily basis. They may sum sales nightly and witness thousands in revenue going through their departments. Corporate executives see the big numbers. They see how profitable individual stores are. They see profit reports on districts and regions. It is important that these people have faith in the company they work for. If they aren't buying their own stock maybe there's a reason why. Maybe profits are falling. Maybe customers aren't coming. Doom and gloom could be near.

But I must admit most mature companies have very little insider ownership. This doesn't mean they aren't good companies. Corporations like Yum and Lockheed-Martin have tiny amounts of insider ownership. It doesn't mean these aren't good stocks. It just means you need to carefully do your research before you invest. Savvy investors won't put all their eggs in one basket anyway. Does anyone remember Enron? Many of Enron's employees lost their entire life's saving when Enron went belly up. They not only lost their primary source of income they lost their retirement too since they participated in Enron's stock purchase program. They put all their eggs in one basket and when they did that they accepted massive risk. For this reason some employees prefer to diversify their savings in many different places and this has no bearing on the health and soundness of the company they work for. I've given you seven great rules to picking good stocks but I must admit I've held back. I'm going to share my eighth rule, my most important rule, for picking good stocks.

My eighth rule, my most important rule, is only invest in companies you understand. You need to understand their business. Too many people lose too much money chasing impossible returns trying to get rich quick. They don't even understand the investments they are buying. Just the other day, I was doing some stock research and ran across a technology company that some stock analyst lauded as the next Microsoft. How many shares did I buy? Zip. None. I didn't purchase a single share. The company's profile lost me on the first few words. It was loaded with acronyms and technical jargon. It was like I was reading Chinese. Despite this stock fitting seven of my eight rules I passed on it. I passed because it failed my most important rule.

The goal here is not to lose money. The goal is to get rich slowly and losing money is counter-productive. It's like trying to walk to the store but instead of walking forward you take steps backwards. The end result is you're never going to get there. That's why I don't compromise on this rule. As a young investor I was burned on the next big thing and I watched my principal evaporate before my eyes. I say to you, right here, right now....Never again!

You must understand an investment that's why I only recommend you invest in companies you know about. I'm talking about companies like McDonald's, Wal-Mart and Lowes. You've eaten their burgers, purchased their goods and visited their garden centers. If you haven't visited a company I wouldn't even invest in them. You know nothing about their operations, how many customers frequent their stores or how good their customer service is. This will eliminate thousands of stocks on the New York Stock Exchange (NYSE). So what, you're not missing out anyway. Most of them are garbage stocks and like great empires of the past; they won't stand the test of time.

Next I need you to look for links to a company's **PROFILE**. On Yahoo! Finance it's on the left side under company information.

The profile provides you with key information to shift through the baloney. In it you'll find information about their core business and how long they have existed. You may find information about their products, size, vision and goals. Most importantly it keeps you on track to adhere to rule eight, the most important rule of all.

Additionally I have to share with you one last thing. Corporations have to file certain reports with the Securities and Exchange Commission (SEC). The two reports you should read in their entirety are the **10-Q Quarterly Report** and the **10-K Annual Report**. By no means should you invest in any stock without reviewing these documents. They provide invaluable insight on the direction a company is going. If you have neither the time, desire or will to critically read these somewhat lengthy reports; I suggest you forget about investing in individual stocks and head for the safer, more secure returns of mutual funds.

Those are my eight rules for stock picking. They have served me well over the course of my life. I don't recommend you follow what I'm saying verbatim nor am I guaranteeing you'll have good results. You are your best financial advisor. Investing in the stock market carries risk and no book or investment strategy can mitigate it completely. However I can say you can't gain anything special without accepting some risk. I took a risk to get my MBA without any guarantees of success. I accepted risk with military service. Walt Disney accepted considerable risk trying to start Disneyland. In fact he went bankrupt but died a very rich man. To get anywhere we must accept risk, we just need to find creative ways to mitigate it.

Chapter 10

You have to learn that your dedication to hard work will pay off. I can promise you that. Because the world loves people who work hard at everything they do. The world notices those people and rewards them for that dedication. It might not be an immediate financial reward, but you will get something.

-Russell Simmons

Never, Ever Sell a Stock

Warren Buffett, the greatest investor of all time has two rules. They are as follows.

Rule #1: Never lose money.

Rule#2: Never forget rule 1.

In order to not lose money you need some sort of strategy. In early 2011, I was talking with my sister about her impending move to Texas from California. She was excited and energetic about her imminent adventure. She enthusiastically chattered about packing, renting a U-Haul truck and Triple A. She talked about her route and babbled on and on about her roadmap.

It dawned on me as we spoke. Investing is like traveling across the country. You have to have a goal. In my sister's case her goal was getting to Texas. In my case my financial goal is a million in cash and assets by 47.

In both goals we require a plan or a roadmap. Think about it hard for a second. Would you really travel across the country without a map? You wouldn't. You'd get lost and you'd never make it provided you didn't have a GPS. There are just too many highways, back roads and interstates.

That's why I'm always surprised by investors that meander through their investment years without a written investment plan. This is just like driving without a map or GPS. You will never reach your goal.

In my case I firmly believe in goal setting. I firmly believe in planning. Planning is part of the investment strategy that is going to get you to the finish line.

I have goals and plans. I have financial goals, relationship goals and career goals. I have short-term goals. I have mid-range goals. I have long-range goals. Goals! You must have goals!

I have plans to achieve the goals too. I plan for the short-term. I plan for the mid-point. I plan for the long-term. Plans! You must have plans.

Your strategy is the product of your plans. It's like the chicken and the egg. The plan comes first and gives birth to the strategy.

If you plan to become a millionaire by 47 years old and you are 18 then you can customize a strategy to achieve your goal in that timeline. Let's say you have the same goal as me, a million by 47 but you're 35 and with no savings. In this case your investment strategy will look totally different from mine.

Each strategy is unique. It is based on a host of variables. These variables include marital status, savings rate, goals, starting principal and projected rates of return on investments.

I want you to know strategies are dynamic, fluid and flexible. You should regularly revisit your investment strategy and update it based on your current performance and the market conditions. For example I think everyone was setback by the 2008-2009 financial crises.

I'm only human and the crisis tugged at my emotions too and I sold some stocks I shouldn't have. I deviated from my strategy and I did it for the wrong reasons. The corporations I was invested in were still fundamentally strong. The companies still paid dividends but I just got caught up in the media hoopla and sold some good stock I shouldn't have.

Luckily I bounced back. I recognized what I was doing and mitigated the damage to my portfolio before it was too late. I deviated from my financial strategy and that isn't a good thing.

When you create your investment strategy you need to take a decent amount of time to figure it out. You need to calculate your financial goals and your timeline to reach them. You need to consider you. You need to figure out how much risk you are ready to accept because your risk tolerance will dictate your plan and therefore your investment strategy.

I suppose we are ready to talk about specifics. Are you ready to hear the details about my strategy? Well here they are.

I mentioned I want to be a millionaire. Doesn't everybody? Well I'm different because I will at some point. I don't talk about dreams; I pursue them. I don't sit and dream; I take action. I'm going to become a millionaire by 47 and retire if I want to and I'm going to do it with a defined strategy to get me to my goal.

I will reach my goal with my core business of buying undervalued real estate. I will supplement my core business with investments in assets. I'm talking about real assets that will pay me money regularly. I'm talking about dividend stocks and bonds.

Here is my actual strategy below. I want you to critically look at it. I want you to debate it among your friends. If you disagree with it I'd love for you to tell me why. If you agree with it feel free to use it for your own purposes. In the following paragraphs I'll talk about each section individually.

Plan constructed: Dec 2010

Plan revised: Feb 2011…no changes were made to the measurable milestones

Vision: Amass wealth for the benefit of my significant others

Mission Statement: Become a millionaire by 47

Objectives:

Short-term: $300K by start of CY2012 (Achieved by early 2011!)

Mid-term: $700K by start of CY2017

Long-term: $1 million in assets by CY2019

Strategy: Purchase distressed real-estate, revamp and hold long-term. Rent out properties to increase current income and increase cash flow for additional investment in stocks and bonds.

Stock/Bond Strategy: Invest 38% of capital in blue-chip stocks paying good dividends/ 39% in high-yield (B-rated or lower) corporate bonds ITO pull 10-20% interest per year. The remaining 23% will be in real estate, short-term cash reserves and a small amount in currencies and precious metals. Paramount to this strategy is rejecting frequent trading based on emotion. Paramount is adopting the strategy of "NEVER SELLING A STOCK/BOND!"

Measurable Milestones:

Graduate Degree by 2011 (increase earning potential)

Year	Balance
1	$294,842.81 - surpassed by early 2011!
2	$372,692.15 - surpassed in late 2011!
3	$467,620.95
4	$583,376.29
5	$724,527.31
6	$896,645.61
7	$1,106,525.13
8	$1,362,450.34

Your strategy is based off your plan. You should initially record the date you constructed your original plan. This date should never change. It reminds you of your persistent purpose toward achieving your goals. It reminds you of how long you've been working at it. In my thoughts this date is really important. It is the date you started doing more than just dreaming. It is the date you started moving towards a defined purpose and stopped wandering aimlessly. In the military we often joke about planning combat. The common phrase is "No plan survives first contact."

This phrase reminds us we must stay open to change. We must be ready to revise and update our initial plan. We should be prepared to scrap our plan completely and start a new one but whatever you do keep that original date because this is the date you took action toward success.

Your plan is a living document. It is subject to change after assets significantly appreciate. It is subject to change if you realize a terrible setback. The only constant in this world is change. So update your plan and strategy regularly. I update mine annually in December. This timeframe gives me a chance to evaluate my investment choices and my return on assets. It gives me a chance to study my current good debt load. It allows me to fully take in the year in review to see where I am and determine where I need to go. Revise your plan and strategy regularly and record the date and move on to your mission.

We must look at vision too. A vision is a broad statement of where you want to be in the future and for what purpose. It is the rationale for your effort. It is designed to answer the nagging questions of why. Why must I budget? Why must I deprive myself of my desires? Why must I invest? In my case it is easy for me to deprive myself. It is easy to be a tight wad. It is easy for me to be frugal. I'm doing it for my children. I want them to inherit my wealth and continue the legacy I've started. I hope that the dollars I earn today through my labor will work for my ancestors for generations to come. Do you see how a vision can provide purpose? Do you see how it can motivate and inspire you when your resolve starts to wane? You must have a vision of what you're trying to achieve and then use individual missions to get there.

I'm a military man. I think in terms of missions about everything. You can't serve 20 plus years in the Air Force and not develop a profound sense of mission. Missions drive everything. We even think of menial tasks like cleaning the bathrooms or vacuuming the floors as missions.

As an officer you are in charge of a lot of enlisted. The enlisted force is our most prized asset. They have unbelievable creativity and ingenuity. I cannot praise them enough. Enlisted men and women have a strong sense of mission and I have had tremendous success communicating with them in terms of the mission. I would often round them up and say to them "I got a mission for you." Or I'd say things like this "We just got a mission from the top." Using these terms I got tremendous action and results.

You must think in terms of mission too. You need to have that same sense of mission that the American serviceman has. He will go into harm's way and never quit until his mission is achieved even against impossible odds. So must you. Develop your mission statement and pursue it with never say quit intensity. Plow through brick walls in pursuit of your mission.

Your mission statement should never really change either. If your mission is to amass a million by 47 and you go broke at 32, I don't think you should adjust your mission. In your plan you just need to figure out a different way to get there. It might entail more risk but I figure if your mission was a million at 47; you are probably not risk adverse. I figure you are probably very comfortable with risk much like I am. Now let's talk about objectives because missions are useless without objectives to move you towards them.

 Goals and objectives are the same thing. They need to be realistic. An unrealistic goal is a fantastic dream. This only results in disappointment for you and reduced self-confidence as you continually fail to reach your goals. Goals and objectives need to be measurable. If they are not measurable, how do you know if you are moving towards your goals? Achieving goals are like winning small battles. Achieving your mission statement is winning the war.

Look at my objectives. They are clear, realistic and measurable. Your goals should be too. Much thought should go into creating them because so much of your future success depends on having desire and great goals. The main course is next. Next is your strategy on how you will achieve your objectives and ultimately your mission.

Your strategy is the culmination of your plans. It must be specific and clear. Before you invest one dollar or purchase any assets; you should think the whole transaction out. You should project return on investment and most importantly ensure you understand it. The asset you purchase "MUST FIT INTO YOUR INVESTMENT STRATEGY!" If it doesn't you must walk away. This will protect your principal from loss. There will be other opportunities in the future and you'll have capital to invest once opportunity coming knocking again. I cannot conclude this chapter without talking about the words that started it. They are in bold print towards the beginning. They are "**Never, Ever Sell a Stock!**" Some might consider this approach controversial. Some might consider it outright dangerous. Some will disregard it completely; some will laugh my beliefs into oblivion.

Some will embrace it. Some will look at my argument with an open mind. Some will experiment with it and many will realize unbelievable profits because it.

To illustrate my point I'm going to use only one example. Let's assume you purchased 100 shares in a great corporation at $10 a share in 1990. It would have cost you $1,000. Let's assume you never purchased another share. Let's say the stock split three times during the 90s. A stock split occurs when a corporation cuts a stock price in half and doubles the amount of your shares. Corporations tend to do this when a stock is rising at a fast pace to encourage continued investment in the company.

Now back to our example. Assuming a 2 to 1 split, your 100 shares become 200 shares on the first split. Your 200 shares become 400 shares on the second split. By the third split your 400 shares becomes 800 shares. Now let's suppose you sold this company today at a current market price of $63.91. What would you have? You would have $51,128; all of this from a $1,000 investment. That's a 5,000% return on investment! Additionally you would have received steady dividend checks every quarter on top of that over the past two decades.

This is the power of buy and hold. This is the power of my strategy of never, ever sell a stock. A stock of this caliber will work for you for generations. If it is a good company it'll work for your descendants too. Many frequent traders dream of being rich but few get there. Why? They trade their stocks too frequently. Their weakness is their emotions. They are slaves to it. Emotions control them; they don't control their emotions and so they fail.

I must offer a disclaimer. This strategy is not risk-free. K-Mart is a great example. At one point K-Mart was the discount store king. I remember there seemed to be K-Marts in every city in America. K-Mart was such a part of American culture some likened it to apple pie.

But K-Mart is a shell of its former self today. Many stores are closed - crowded out by the growth of Wal-Mart. A market share K-Mart once ruled. If a person brought and held K-Mart for the long haul much of their principal would be gone today but regular dividend payments would have prevented a total loss. In fact it's likely you'd have regained your initial investment long before the iconic retail store faded. I really wish I could provide you with a risk-free approach to getting rich but there isn't one. You will have risk. You just need to find ways to reduce it.

I implore you not to get hung up on the daily fluctuations of stocks. Stocks go up and down but there overall direction is up over the long-term. All too often people sit glued to computer screens watching the daily fluctuation of stocks from opening to closing bell all in an effort to make a few dollars. These people let life pass by because they're obsessed with money and the false happiness they think it can bring. When I purchase stocks I purchase great corporations with great management and I forget about them. The daily fluctuations don't matter to me because I know I've purchased a real asset that will continually pay me. I suppose if I purchased speculative stocks that don't pay dividends I'd stay glued to the computer or the tube more but I usually don't. Proven companies with proven track records reduce risk and lower the risk of an anxiety attack too.

The strategy of never-ever selling a stock works for the most part but you need to do good research prior to locking in your buy order. Use my rules or develop your own. Understand your purchases and pour over SEC filings. Do detailed research first and own the stock for life. The greatest investor in the world is largely a buy and hold guy. You probably should be too.

Chapter 11

Save a part of your income and begin now, for the man with a surplus controls circumstances, and the man without a surplus is controlled by circumstances.

-Henry Buckley

Consumer Credit

I cannot write a guide about personal finance, financial independence or whatever you want to call it without addressing consumer credit in greater detail. Consumer credit is one of the greatest inhibitors to financial success. It saps you of your future income and you need every dollar you can muster to work for you. It is especially important for low income earners to reject consumer credit altogether. Before I get on my soapbox let me define consumer credit in my own words.

I define consumer credit as any type of credit used to purchase non-assets. Earlier I defined an asset as anything that pays you money regularly. Remember that? Another word for non-assets is junk. Junk doesn't pay you money regularly no matter how valuable you THINK it is. Some will argue with me about assets such as small capitalization stocks and growth stocks that don't pay dividends. Okay I concede the point. Small caps and growth stocks can rise in value but they can fall just as well. That's why I still don't consider these investment vehicles assets. I know the diehards want to keep this argument going so let's continue then. They'll say "But large capitalization stocks can fall in value too so they aren't assets either." The great debaters will raise their arms in the air confident of victory but I'll counter once more before I throw in the towel.

Small cap stocks don't put money in your pocket. If these stocks paid dividends, if they sent you a regular check, rise or fall they'd be assets. They'd generate income for you. Even if you sit on your behind and watch old reruns of "The Smurfs"; you'd still get paid. This is what separates dividend payers from all other investments. That's why dividend stocks are the only stocks I advocate. My own portfolio it's loaded with dividend paying stocks. I may own a few small caps or growth stocks but I don't think the average investor should. It's better to own an asset that pays you. Let's get back to consumer credit.

All consumer credit is bad debt. Let me list some things people regularly purchase with consumer credit so you get an idea of what I'm talking about. This is my DO NOT buy on credit list. Of course you can purchase these items but only buy them with cash and with your 85% allocation. If you can't do that you need to save for them. If you can't purchase these items with 85% of your income and you can't save for them; I suppose you'll just have to do without these consumer goods. I'm so against purchasing any of these items with consumer credit; I'm going to format each item in a Thou Shall NOT list. Here we go:

Thou Shall NOT purchase a car on credit.
Thou Shall NOT purchase furniture on credit.
Thou Shall NOT take vacations on credit.
Thou Shall NOT purchase cost of living expenses on credit (i.e. gas, food, household item, etc).
Thou Shall NOT purchase restaurant meals on credit.
Thou Shall NOT purchase luxuries on credit (i.e. jewelry, hot tub, foot massager, etc).

Wow! I like how this is going so let me continue.

Thou Shall NOT have a credit card if you are a low income earner.
Thou Shall NOT have more than one credit card.

Right now readers across the world are yelling "Who does this guy think he is?" If you give me a second I'll explain each one of my commandants.

A car is one of the worst purchases you can make on credit. It immediately depreciates the moment you drive it off the lot. It's usually not a small depreciation either. On average a $25,000 car will depreciate $3,750 in the first year. That is 15%! Now let's say you got a "great" loan. Let's say you borrowed $25,000 at 10%. In this example you probably had some past credit problems and the loan company was gracious enough to help you rebuild your credit. In the first year you are already down 25%! That's 15% in depreciation and another 10% in interest payments. That's 25% of your hard earned cash gone when you combine the depreciation loss with the interest expenses. You see where I'm going with this. The depreciation loss doesn't stop there. It continues year after year. You're wealth is disappearing before your eyes.

Automobiles are consumer goods. This means automobiles do not last forever. This means they aren't one time indestructible purchases. Automobiles wear out. They are meant to be consumed.

Automobiles don't add to your wealth. They take away from it. If you are like the typical American you pay interest on your auto loan, you pay for gasoline, you pay for maintenance and you pay for upkeep like carwashes.

You pay all the time and regularly. Automobiles cost you enough there is no need for additional interest expenses because you brought your dream car on credit.

Who can purchase a new car with cash? The answer is not many of us not even me. I have hundreds of thousands of dollars and I still can't afford to purchase a new car with cash. Well, let me restate that, I CHOOSE not to purchase a new car with cash. I'm seeking financial independence. I'm seeking financial security and purchasing a new car with cash isn't consistent with my goals. Even people with considerable stored wealth have limits.

In reality only a few Americans can afford a brand new car. The average American should purchase a used vehicle with cash. Do not spend more than two months of your net income on a car. If you are a minimum wage worker earning $1,100 monthly; you should spend no more than $2,200. If you earn $6000 a month, you can spend up to $12,000 but purchase this car with cash. If it takes you a couple of months to save up for it then wait! Do not purchase automobiles with credit. Consumer credit is like a fire. It can start out small but if unchecked it grows and rages out of control. Reject purchasing cars on credit. See them for what they really are; just more consumer junk.

Furniture often gets many people into trouble. It even got me in trouble when I was young. Alas, I was a young man unwise in the handling of money. I was recently married and I wanted to provide my beautiful wife all the "good" things in life. I found us a one-bed room apartment in the shady side of town in Warner Robins, Georgia and I rushed to the furniture store to furnish it.

Instead of buying used furniture I went to the new stuff. I picked out this contemporary brown couch with black stripes. It came with a matching love seat and three black and gold coffee tables. I was the man. The salesman quoted me a price for the entire set. Money was no object. I had credit. I had good credit.

I filled out a promissory note, quickly shook hands with the furniture salesman and the deal was struck. My modern living room furniture was delivered within a few days.

It was great resting on the flashy furniture but over time things happened. A spilled juice cup here and an accidental tear there. Pretty soon it no longer looked like the furniture I remembered and loaded with newly-wed expenses, I was still paying on it. I noticed I was making very little progress on paying it off too.

Frustrated with my progress towards paying it off, I got a second job and paid off all my debts within three months. I sacrificed a lot of free time to get myself out of debt. I sacrificed sleep and sleep is important to me. I was already working 40 hours a week on my first job and I tacked on an additional 20. I sacrificed career progression and education. I had no time to study for promotion or pursue an advanced degree. I sacrificed leisure but most of all, I sacrificed time with my lovely wife.

I think back on that event. I'm divorced now and I lost critical time with a loved one and for what. All over a couch that's probably in a landfill somewhere hosting a colony of termites. It's ironic really, the happiness that furniture brought me was so short-lived but the time I lost working for material possessions was eternal.

In 2009, I went to Six Flags over Texas during record heat. The temperature was so hot all I wanted to do was find shade, any shade. I stomped angrily between thrill rides. I wanted to be anywhere but there. Outside - In the blistering heat! The only thing that would have made this vacation any worst was if I brought it on credit.

Vacations on credit are no-nos. Sure you'll have lasting memories but the fallout to financial independence is too much. This is especially true for really expensive retreats like a family cruise or a trip to Disneyland. These are usually once in a lifetime events requiring careful planning to limit expenses and maximize fun. Vacations purchased on credit are usually resented by the borrower in the future. As the bills arrive, memories of $10 soft-drinks and a $40 picture of you on the Tornado thrill ride doesn't seem grand at all. I want you to take vacations but not regret it later. If you pay with cash the chances of you regretting your vacation is much less than if you don't.

I once knew a guy so overwhelmed by credit card debt; he was forced to buy essentials like food on credit. He spiraled further and further into the credit abyss. Eventually he lost his home due to foreclosure. He became another statistic reported on during nightly news updates on the economy.

If you get to the point where you have to purchase essentials on credit; you are in serious trouble. Your spending habits have brought you to the brink of self-destruction and you need serious help. You need debt relief 9-1-1. Once you are forced to purchase one morsel of food on credit, stop what you are doing and seek professional help because you are officially on a very slippery slope and with one false move you are going to go tumbling down. You have to have essentials like food. This is a basic need but if you're buying food on credit expect your debt to grow unabated without skilled intervention from a debt professional.

If you're like me you purchase the same dish from your favorite restaurant every time. You want to try new stuff but you want to avoid a disappointing dish. Now imagine you've waited all month to go to your favorite steakhouse. You look at your favorite dish, Rib-Eye steak with mashed potatoes. You think to yourself "Oh, that steak is so good but I get it every time; maybe I should try something new." You silently continue thinking to yourself. You conclude you are adventurous and commit yourself to something new. You order the blue-ribbon baby-back ribs. It was the "blue-ribbon" that caught your attention. If they are "blue-ribbon" the ribs have to be good! You order the ribs and after waiting what seems an eternity; the ribs arrive at the table. They look good. They smell good but the first bite confirms that they are awful. They are so dry; the Sahara Desert seems like the Indian Ocean. You choke down bite after bite until the $30 dinner is gone. Is there anything more terrible than this meal? Yes. What if you were already in financial trouble and you brought this disaster on credit? Dining out can be fun but a meal isn't an asset. The only things you are approved to buy with debt are real assets.

Luxuries will get you in trouble. The world is filled with wonderful junk. I'm talking about high-tech foot massagers and the latest knick-knack. This kind of junk is okay to own. In fact I encourage you to spend a little and enjoy life some. It makes little sense to hoard every dollar you earn. But YOU SHOULDN'T BUY THESE THINGS ON CREDIT. You must pay for this junk with your 85%. If you can't pay for it with the 85% you should save up for it or do without. Junk comes and goes, it fact, my garage is loaded with it. I try not to think about all the long hours I worked for that stuff. My only comfort is the majority of it was purchased by my ex-wife. The fact remains I would be so much richer today if I never brought that junk.

Before you purchase any luxuries I want you to think about how many hours you'll have to work to pay for it. If you still want it and you have available cash to buy it; I want you to wait a week and think about it. If you still want it you should buy it provided you don't put yourself in a pickle. Luxuries are a part of life. All men desire things but remember all men cannot satisfy every desire so careful thought should go into all expenditures. Luxuries are ok. It is great to own and enjoy nice things but luxuries are never, ever permissible on credit.

All the minimum wage earners in the house say "Hey!" All the minimum wage earners in the house say "Ho!" Say "Hey!" Say "Ho!" Are you singing along?

If you earn minimum wage it is important to know who you are. It is important to know your limitations. If you earn minimum wage you need to be especially careful. It is so easy for you to get caught up in inescapable debt and so difficult for you to pay it off once you do. That's why I recommend you stay 12 feet away from any credit card. YOU DON'T NEED ONE! A lot of people are surprised when I say this. These same people would argue a credit card is required for emergencies. I've lived virtually my whole life without a credit card. I only recently got one and I didn't get it for financial security. I got it for the nice rewards program. I still immediately pay off every purchase I make on my credit card within hours after I make it. I get the reward points and I don't incur any bad debt.

All credit cards carry higher interest rates; even the ones, with a nice introductory 2% APR. It is important to read the small print on that contract you are about to sign and focus on the word "introductory." This type of card is like a siren singing the sweetest songs as you strain to resist her as you pass by. These financial companies are friendly enough to allow you to transfer all that bad debt you've racked up by owning and using several different credit cards. Unfortunately the fine print shows it ugly face again. The nice 2% introductory interest rate only lasts for three months and then it jumps up to a whopping 18%! The song doesn't sound so sweet anymore huh. Credit cards are time bombs ready to explode and minimum wage earners should stay completely away from them! Resist that lady in Wal-Mart promising you a free bag of chips for completing the credit card application. More people than you realize struggle with consumer debt and low income earners are the most vulnerable. A step in the wrong direction leads you down the wrong road, overwhelmed and underwater, struggling for air.

What if I earn much more than minimum wage? I can have a credit card right? I can have many credit cards right?

Credit cards are extremely dangerous even for high income earners. As people earn more money; their toys simply get bigger. Instead of a set of roller blades; they buy a speed boat for fun. Instead of a trip to a neighboring city for a vacation; they are off the Jamaica. A large income doesn't necessary mean large wealth. Middle and upper class earners must cautiously exploit credit to their own advantage. These earners still must budget, monitor expenses, save and invest to increase cash flow. To responsibility manage their credit lines I recommend a person have no more than one open line of credit. I know this is a revolutionary concept for some but I've lived this way my entire life and it has served me quite well.

This concludes my bashing of credit. Financial institutions around the world are clenching their teeth and declaring jihad. Large banks and credit unions are massive institutions continually flexing their financial muscle with deep coffers to fund effective advertising campaigns but just like little David defeated Goliath so will I confidently take on the credit industry. Credit for junk obstructs your bottom-line and just because everyone else is doing it doesn't mean you have to. Reject all forms of consumer credit and only use credit to purchase assets not junk. Real assets put cash in your pockets until they bulge and overflow. Credit cards don't do that!

Chapter 12

Thoughts are the thermostat that regulates what we accomplish in life. My body responds and reacts to input from my mind. If I feed my mind upon doubt, disbelief and discouragement, that is precisely the kind of day my body will experience. If I adjust my thermostat forward to thoughts filled with vision, vitality and victory, I can count on that kind of day.

-Charles Swindoll

Putting it all together

This is the chapter where we take the entire book and its principals and apply it to a real world situation. This is where we prove or disprove the theory. This is where we separate fact from fiction, the men from the boys. This is where someone who wants wealth suffers and sacrifices for it. This example is based on a true story and the proceedings are based on actual events.

In our case study we have a 62 year old woman, living in Los Angeles, California earning $1100 monthly. She is working part-time and earning a little over minimum wage. Her first step towards putting it all together is for her to fix HERSELF mentally.

She needs desire to want something better first or no book in the world can help her. She needs to want a better lot in life. She wakes up on a Saturday morning after a restless night's sleep and commits to change and reaching her full potential even at her advanced age. She reviews her life and sees her mistakes and commits to learn from them. She appraises her past earnings throughout her lifetime and looks around with contempt at her humble surroundings and is determined to achieve something better. SHE HAS A STRONG, BURNING DESIRE AND THIS IS THE FIRST STEP.

Number 1, she has desire so there is hope. Next she gets a copy of this book. After reading it page for page she pledges herself to the wisdom it provides. She takes out a pencil and does the math and consigns herself to live on 85% of her income, a humble $935 a month. Next she lists all of her expenses and her meager sources of income. She evaluates all her expenditures and decides to cut costs. She vows to go line by line and eliminate any fat she finds. She starts with her rent. Her rent is

$300. Actually it is $800 but she is on Section 8. She pays $300 and the government supplements the other $500. She always dreamt of being assistance free. She has a burning desire for 100% independence, beholden to none.

She sees little possibility of achieving that dream in Los Angeles. Tremendous demand in the rental market is outpacing supply causing rental costs to soar. Home ownership is completely out of reach for her too in California and renting aid free is impossible at the present time. She gives her dilemma careful thought over several months and chooses to move to Texas.

She chooses a place to settle called Copperas Cove. It is a suburban, family town with scarcely 35, 000 people. It is a bustling small city, relatively untouched by crime. It is the type of city used for a taping of the "Leave It to Beaver" show. It is a model of what America once was; nostalgic communities with strong values where good conquers bad and right triumphs over wrong.

She finds this place over the internet. On a website called bestplaces.net. She compares key statistics like job growth, crime and cost-of-living. She visits the town and marvels at its strong economy and peaceful living. The largest military post in the world is just 10 miles from her new spot and this community has hardly felt the recession. This is the place she chooses to call home.

Her only funds are the proceeds from her last year's tax return. Never looking back she sells all her furniture, quits her job and purchases a one way ticket to Texas through Expedia.com for $300. Once the airplane touches down in Texas she hits the ground running. Without a home she shacks up with her son, a military officer who happens to be stationed there temporarily. With shelter secured her first priority is a car.

Her son drives her around. The strategy they use is the same strategy the government uses to award government contracts. By using this strategy they likely can effectively judge market prices and get the car they are looking for at a fair price. They select at least three car dealerships each having the same car they are looking for. After consultation with her son she chooses a 1998 Ford Taurus. She chooses this car based on her income, she was determined to spend no more than two times her monthly pay ($2200) on transportation. American cars are usually less expensive since they are not affected by import tariffs and maintenance costs are less since parts are often abundant.

She finds a really clean car at the first lot. The car is in fantastic shape. Its white paint job seems to sparkle in the sun. The interior is clean and freshly detailed and mechanically it is sound. They haggle persistently to get the lowest price and finally settle in at about $4000. This is much more than two times her income so she files the written price quote in her purse and moves on.

The next lot she finds the exact same car. This time it is gray. There is some body damage; a dent by the tail light on the passenger side. The interior is well-worn. The mechanical condition is highly suspect because the car won't even start. Disappointed with this prospect she moves on. She wonders if this strategy will work. She wonders if she will ever find a decent car within her budget.

She only had two dealers scheduled today. On a whim she stops at a third dealer on the way home. He has a 1998 Ford Taurus in stock. He shows her the car. The exterior is in good condition. There are scratches in the paint job, some worn spots but the body is damage-free. The car starts promptly. The engine is quiet and seems to hum a sweet tune to the ear. Her son looks under the bottom for visible leaks and finds none. They take it for a test drive. The vehicle handles smoothly, effortlessly taking corners with ease and easily accelerating to highway speeds. Mechanically the vehicle is good to go but the air conditioning doesn't work. The hot Texas sun begins to take its toll on the passengers and they rapidly roll down the windows to let in the hot, breezy air. It is refreshing but they still need to take the lack of air conditioning into consideration.

After returning to the car lot they start to haggle about the price but the dealer doesn't have any of it. They are a deep discount auto dealer buying autos at auction, slapping a profitable markup on them and selling them to the public without compromising their markup. It really is an efficient business model since you have virtually no sells staff.

He says to her bluntly, "The price of the car is $2100." "This price includes tax, title and registration. Take it or leave it."

The son and mother smile to each other and nod their heads in unison. The mom virtually yells out for all in the shop to hear "I'll take it!"

With a car secured she looks for work. Inspired by desire she finds it quickly. Within two weeks of unpacking she finds employment at Wal-Mart. She is hired as a jewelry associate. The position fits well with her abilities and interests. Even as a little kid she loved the sparkle of polished gold. In her advanced years stocking jobs would have been to labor intensive for her. She is thankful for fast employment with a good corporation.

With her strong desire and tremendous work ethic she survives the training program which was difficult for her. She was a high school drop-out with little computer experience. She didn't complete her GED until she was in her 50s but fueled by desire she completes the training program and is immediately awarded a raise based on her experience and performance. DESIRE IS A POWERFUL ENTITY!

Her son isn't a chip off the old block. He is a college graduate a stone's throw from his graduate degree. He is a prodigious accumulator of wealth and has hundreds of thousands in cash and assets. He talks in-depth about "unhealthy desires." Things like greed and want and the false satisfaction spending brings. He explains the 85% method and after hours of instruction; more and more, she likes what she hears. Knowing she has nothing to lose she commits herself to the program.

She targets 85% of her net income for living expenses. It works out to $935. She opens a checking account and signs up for direct deposit over the internet but she is missing something. She misses her independence and longs for a home of her own. She finds a quaint home for rent on the lower economic side of town. The neighborhood is quiet and the children well-behaved. She negotiates with the property manager and the deal is struck. She's able to acquire the house for 30% of her income or $330. This is higher than the 20% the plan calls for but she really wants this house so she takes it anyway. With housing secured she continues following the plan.

The plan calls for an emergency fund to effectively deal with life's hiccups. By now living on 85% is no longer hard for her. She has developed a habit for saving and she finds great pleasure in logging onto her banking accounts and seeing actual money in there. In accordance with the plan she establishes a new account to store emergency funds. She chooses a regular checking account and auto-transfers $55 or 5% of her net income to the account monthly. Each day she logs-in and watches with pleasure as her emergency fund rises month by month.

The plan targets 10% of her net income to long-term saving. The $110 is automatically transferred. It was difficult to adjust to it at first but with drive, motivation and inspiration she makes it work. What to do with this 10% is a difficult question at this point? Most mutual funds require a $3,000 minimum balance so mutual funds are out of reach for her at the moment and saving accounts earn pathetic interest and she needs safety because she is risk adverse. Vanguard's set of mutual funds can help but alas she is a minimum wage earner and $110 won't open a brokerage account with them. How can she invest with such a tiny amount?

Her son is very financial savvy. He seems to know it all, home-buying, investing and taxes. He points her to an investment vehicle that's as diversified as a mutual fund and is traded on the NYSE. He points her to an Exchange-Traded Fund (ETFs). ETFs are just like mutual funds but they trade in real-time on the New York Stock Exchange. They are more stable than most stocks because of their diversity. Some dividend paying ETFs provide nice income too.

In $500 blocks she chooses to invest in a diversified, income generating ETF. The ETF she purchases is from a reputable brokerage company and all of the holdings are big-name corporations. The fund holds leading corporations like McDonalds, Yum Corporation and Proctor and Gamble to name a few. After purchasing the first asset in her life she celebrates downtown with a steak dinner at her favorite restaurant.

After three months the dividend checks start rolling it. The $3.75 payment is small but she rejoices at receiving what feels like free money. She recognizes the value of reinvesting her dividends. With a smile on her face and new determination in her soul, she drifts off to sleep and dreams of great riches.

A year passes and she has paid herself faithfully. She has amassed $1452 in ETFs. Pleased by her results she continues the habit and talks about the plan to anyone who will listen.

In this case we looked at an actual testimony of this plan. Before the plan this individual would blow through $5,000 tax returns and struggle for food to eat later in the year. This undisciplined consumer spent her way into a vicious cycle of work and pay bills. Living paycheck to paycheck was a way of life but look at her now. She pays herself first and reinvests the dividends. Her personal wealth is growing without aid from others or a handout. She has food to eat and a comfortable place to sleep. She is just getting started but this is the power of the plan. It transformed her from an unwise spender to a shrewd saver. Her personal wealth is climbing as she grows her asset column. If she continues this plan unabated the results will be shocking.

If she stays the course after 10 years her accounts will swell to $26,907.25 assuming a 10% return on investment. If she stays the course for 20 years she'll have $92, 931.63 assuming she stays consistent with her $110 deposits and a 10% return on investment is achieved from her various investment platforms. This is the undeniable power of compounding. It is an incredible force achieving amazing results. One must wonder why all don't practice it. The truth of financial independence has been presented to you. Deny it if you dare, cradle to grave labor will be your reward.

Every month our case study still needs to study her cash flow. She must track what goes out and what comes in. Once she receives more income monthly from assets than she spends; she is officially rich by this book. She can work or not work at this point. The choice is hers and hers alone.

Our case study rejects consumer credit cards 100%. In fact she carries no debt whatsoever. In her eyes every dollar is critical and when dollars disappear they can't work for you. She sacrifices a lot and denies herself much but her dreams of financial security are becoming more and more of a reality as the days carry on.

Our case study is wary of her friends. She surrounds herself with people with similar values and thoughts like hers. Ambitious people getting the most out of life; her old sets of negative, idle friends are washed away.

One last thing, our case study is cautious of family. She absorbs and analyzes their words and rejects their attempts to take advantage of her. She has the wisdom of years and she sees straight through envy, jealousy and greed. She is mindful of those who will take advantage of her especially her children and grandchildren. She whispers to herself "My earnings are mine to keep" and goes about her daily activities with a smile on her face and happiness in her soul.

Chapter 13

When you have a number of disagreeable duties to perform, always do the most disagreeable first.

-Anonymous

What if I'm in debt now?

Life and debt - It seems we can't have one without the other huh. By now I hope you've brought into my philosophy about debt. I hope you realize debt is not necessarily a bad thing when used for the right purpose.

It's ok to assume debt in an effort to earn more money. Businesses do it all the time in the form of leverage. With personal debt you must be very careful how much debt you assume even if it is for an approved purpose.

I use a couple of ratios to keep me in-control of my "good" debt. First I use a debt to asset ratio. With this calculation I divide my debt against my assets. My rule is to keep this ratio at 15% or below. I recently completed an acquisition of an investment property. My current debt to assets ratio is 28%. This acquisition drove my debt to assets ratio above my comfortable threshold. I will not complete any further acquisitions until it drops below my acceptable threshold. Strict adherence to your investment strategy is a must. It is the difference between the poor house and the big house. All too often promising individuals and promising companies are destroyed because of greed. They taste success and they try to grow too fast, too large, too quickly. The slow path to riches is more gratifying and the road is less dangerous. Wealth that comes quickly is quickly lost. Ask the penniless former lottery winners if what I say isn't true.

The second ratio I use is my expense to income ratio. With this ratio I tally all my expenses and divide it against all forms of my income. This includes things like rental property, royalties, web site revenue, a salary and dividend payments. For this figure my rule is to keep my expense to income ratio below 28%. Anything else is too much in my opinion and you begin accepting larger risk. Use your net income to calculate this figure. Taxes are taken before you ever touch the money so it's senseless to use gross income. My current expense to income ratio is 28%. This is at my upper limit. I will not assume any more new expenses until my expense to income ratio falls below 28%. This is my rule and I'm sticking to it.

Let us assume you brought this book and believe in it and are ready to take the path to financial independence but you are in debt. What do you do? Read on and find out because I have techniques to get you out of debt and it doesn't include filing for bankruptcy.

The first thing you need to do is commit yourself to mastering your situation. The path I offer isn't easy. It is a hard road. You'll have to deny yourself many of the so-called pleasures in life to eliminate your debt. Your standard of living will change incredibly. Ask yourself "Am I committed to this?" You need to reaffirm your commitment because I believe the alternative I offer you for paying off your debt is probably harder than other choices like bankruptcy. There's a hard road and an easier one. Paying off your debts with my plan is the hard one. Bankruptcy may be easier but I would never recommend that. An honest person pays all their debts. I guarantee the alternative I offer you is more rewarding than bankruptcy. Paying off your debts honorably leaves you with confidence and independence. You'll be respected among men and valued by your family. Many people will be happy to call you friend. I hope you "man up" and choose the hard road and pay off your debts. For people in debt I recommend you not live off 85% of your income.

For people in debt I recommend you cover all of your living expenses with 65% of your earnings. Wow! Really?

Living off 65% of your income will take incredible changes. You may have to change apartments or even sell your home. You may even need to sell your vehicle and ride the city bus but this is the only way to conquer your debts. If you live off 65% of your income you will free up 20% to provide to your creditors and still store 5% for an emergency fund and 10% for long-term savings. I shudder to think about how hard it must be to live off of 65% of your income but I know it can be done. How? I know it can be done because others have done it before you. Despite what you may believe you are not a special case. Many others in this country have struggled with debt. Many have conquered it and you will too if you are committed. Let's work this plan with an example using actual numbers.

Let's assume a 29 year old woman named Jane is about $11,000 in debt and she earns minimum wage. Let's say her last name is Doe. You knew that was coming huh?

Many financial experts would encourage Jane to aggressively attack her debt but here's where I differ and here's why. Attacking Jane's debt aggressively doesn't fix Jane mentally. She still is the same old Jane. She will just be a debt-free Jane and since she hasn't changed mentally she will quickly find herself in debt once again as soon as her spending returns. No. The proper way to solve this problem is to fix Jane mentally and making Jane pay herself first is a start. Using this plan Jane develops a habit of saving. This is a real culture shift from what Jane once was, an out-of-control spender. Alright let's look at the numbers.

Jane's income is $1160 monthly. Using the plan she must live off of 65% or $754. I stated earlier housing costs should be no more than 20% of your income or $232 in this case. That leaves Jane $522 to live on. She'll need to pay for food, clothing, utilities, auto insurance, telephone and gasoline. Depending of the size of Jane's apartment this might be possible or Jane may have to move to a cheaper place. Additionally Jane must research and tap into federal programs to assist low-income with utilities and telephone communications. If she does this, she will maximize her available cash to live on and free up cash to pay down her debts. Jane has several different options to pay off her debt.

Depending on her level of debt she can approach it in different ways. She can aggressively attack it one bill at a time starting with the highest interest debt first. I only recommend this approach if she already defaulted on some personal debt and maintaining her current credit score just isn't possible. Using this approach she attacks each debt one at a time. With time her debts will fade and creditors will get their just payments.

As in this case when someone is overwhelmed with debt they must contact every one of their creditors and explain the situation. Ask them to reduce or suspend interest rates. Often creditors will rather lose some interest payments than lose their principal completely. Sometimes creditors will offer lump sum pay offs at considerable discounts. You never know what is available until you ask.

Another approach Jane may take is aggressively attacking her highest interest debt with extra principal. Then she can make minimum payments on all the rest. One by one she'll eliminate her debts starting with the highest interest debt first. This approach increases her credit rating and avoids bankruptcy. With this approach she faces her debts head-on and regains control over them.

I presented you two approaches to eliminating debt each equally painful but for some there are options now. For those in debt you got yourself into this; now get yourself out. Your brain will help you. That gooey stuff between your ears is the same gooey stuff responsible for tremendous human creations like space flight and solar power. Your brain has infinite potential should you choose to develop and use it. Do you really think your brain can't solve your debt problem?

I implore you to take the hard road and reconstruct your budget. You will find the surplus cash you need provided you're willing to sacrifice and make hard choices. I recommend the hard road less traveled. It will fix you mentally and you will develop strong, wealth accumulating habits and that's something bankruptcy can't do for you!

Chapter 14

Every man like myself, who never went to college, can largely make up for that lack by reading the wise sayings of the great men of the past, who gladly left their wisdom and experience in proverbs for us who follow them.

-Sir Winston Churchill

Choosing friends

Everyone wants friends. People are social creatures. We like being around others. Our times with family and friends seem to be the happiest. A lot of men and women will attest to this statement.

But sometimes it is better to NOT have friends. Why I would recommend such an anti-social stance?

There are good friends and there are bad ones. Let's start on a positive note with good friends. Good friends genuinely care about your well-being. One-time a good friend of mine had too much to drink at a party. He was slightly tipsy but his motor skills were still sharp. At the end of the event he declared his intent to drive home. I suspected him under the influence and refused to allow him to drive home. After much discussion I convinced him to surrender his keys and I drove him home myself. This is genuinely caring about a friend's well-being. There was no chance of reward or profit for me. I just cared about a friend; a friend who was going to make a serious mistake. He could've been arrested or worst he could've killed someone. If a person claims to be your friend, friends won't let friends break the law, hurt themselves or hurt others. Next is an example of a not so good friend.

I dated this girl once. She was a bartender. She would often work late since this particular nightclub closed around two in the morning. After months of working this job she decided to quit. Her profession induced a lot of stress in our relationship. The whole bartender thing just didn't fit into my lifestyle. So in an effort to save our relationship; she left her job.

After providing ample notice to her managers, she was working her last shift at the club. The other bartenders, waitresses, bouncers and greeters all claimed her as a "friend." They celebrated their "friendship" and her last night on the job with jello-shot after jello-shot. She quickly became intoxicated. She announced her intention to drive home after her shift and NOT ONE PERSON PROTESTED!

This young lady was visibly drunk and smelled of alcohol and NOT ONE OF HER "FRIENDS" PROTESTED! With friends like that, who needs enemies?

This story did not end well for this young lady. On her way home there was a bumper-to-bumper traffic jam. Intoxicated and bored, she fell asleep waiting for traffic to move. She awoke to the bright flashing lights of a police cruiser and the traffic ahead of her was long gone.

The officer tapped on her window and collected her papers and checked her driver's license. When he stuck his head inside her window to grab the documents, he caught the unmistakable odor of alcohol. This was the beginning of the end for her.

Her slurred speech and poor motor skills confirmed his suspicions and after a field sobriety test the police officer had seen enough and arrested her on the spot. She was probably too intoxicated to understand her Miranda Rights. Embarrassed and ashamed, she was hauled off to jail.

Not only did she lose her freedom for a while this girl lost me. Her actions and values sparked me to end the relationship. All of this may have been avoided with better judgment on her part and "real friends" that really cared about her well-being.

Despite meaningless and fake words to the contrary, her "friends" were not friends. These people didn't care for her well-being or safety at all. True friends just can't let friends do stupid, dangerous stuff.

In a different example I deployed to a military conflict in 2007. I left behind a wife and two small children. While I was thousands of miles away my wife became ill. After an examination by a physician she was ordered to remain in the hospital for evaluation. My wife was in the hospital for days and I was light years away and my two small children needed adult supervision and care. We didn't know what to do.

One of my co-workers stepped up to help me in my time of need. He and his wife cared for my children as if they were their own. It was a really selfless act of kindness because they were under no obligation to do it. They were just good hearted people. This is a good example of choosing good friends with good traditional values. The important thing is your friends need to be POSITIVE EXAMPLES. To paraphrase Tyler Perry, "YOU CAN DO BAD ALL BY YOURSELF, YOU DON'T NEED ANY HELP!" This is such a powerful statement and it's so true. Life is hard enough you don't need anyone to bring you down. As soon as someone displays self-destructive characteristics, YOU MUST REMOVE

YOURSELF FROM THE SITUATION. You must MAKE THE HARD DECISION AND CEASE BEING THAT PERSON'S FRIEND! You must do this for your own sanity, safety and well-being. I don't know you but if you are in this situation I beg you to follow my advice and remove that person from your inner circle. Quite frankly they don't deserve the privilege of being your friend.

Wisely choose friends. With healthy friends you can reach the stars. With unhealthy ones you can dissipate into a black hole. Anyone who ever achieved greatness didn't do it with negative people by their side. Negativity breeds unhappiness, anger and contempt. It is the root of everything evil in one's life. Things like low self-esteem, lack of confidence, depression and misery.

Positive friends are the catapult to prosperity. With positive friends you will have intelligent conversations and spend what seems like endless hours mapping out your futures. You'll be happier and less angry. Emotions like misery and contempt will still happen but they'll be largely short-lived. It is so difficult to stay upset when your frown is met with a smile. You will find their positive outlook infectious.

Look hard at your current inner circle. Are you surrounding yourself with the right people? Are you choosing your friends wisely? Are your values agreeable? Does their presence really make you happy?

These are tough questions, requiring tough unbiased answers. Many dictionaries don't know the definition of a "friend", do you?

Chapter 15

I don't know the key to success, but the key to failure is trying to please everyone.

-Bill Cosby

Choosing a mate

Behind every good man is a good woman. This statement is the undeniable truth. When a man has a woman it makes him approach every day with tremendous vitality but if he is single is he doomed to mediocrity? No.

It is better to remain single then choose a mate unwisely. For example a chronic saver and a habitual spender are doomed to failure. It may not happen today or tomorrow but trust me the end of that relationship is coming.

It is important you choose your mate wisely because failed relationships are often costly. In my divorce settlement I had to pay out of the wazoo to get it done. I signed over a quarter of my net worth at the time. I gave up a car. I gave up investment portfolios. I gave up alimony. Overall $60,000 disappeared in a short period. It was hard watching it go.

This was my burden for choosing the wrong spouse. She was a spender. I'm a saver. She was negative. I'm more optimistic. She wasn't ambitious. I strive for achievement. We were so different.

I'm trying to highlight the importance of commonality in your mate. You should share similar goals, values and personality if you intend for your relationship to stand the test of time.

Rushing into marriage or a domestic partnership may be costly in the future if you choose wrong. You may pay more than money too. You may pay in mental anguish, happiness and lost time and that is a hefty price.

I know many men entangled by beautiful, high-maintenance women. These men work until their backs break while their women spend and spend. These men drive old clunkers while their women cruise in the current year automobile. All the while he works and works; one job, maybe two, maybe more.

I've visited their homes. They have stuff everywhere. The majority of the stuff was purchased by their husband's labor. Perhaps some will read this book and conclude I have anger issues and resentment towards women but I want to say I don't. I respect women and I recognize we need each other but high-maintenance PEOPLE (both men and women) are my beef. High-maintenance PEOPLE detract from financial security. I don't know about you but I refuse to work until my back breaks. I chose unwisely once but I've learned from the past. Scripture tells us a man and a woman should be equally yoked. What does that mean? It simply means they should be similar in some ways. A saver and spender will have tremendous conflict at some point in their relationship but two spenders will likely happily spend their way into oblivion. Two hoarders will love hoarding last year's goat cheese together but a hoarder and one who hates clutter will be at each other's throat.

That is all I'm saying. I'm a straight shooter and I call it how it is. I'm the first to admit every great person has had a great spouse by their side.

I'm single at 38 years old. I was married once and the divorce nearly sent me to the poor house. It took me over two years of careful saving and investing to replace what I lost. There are many others out there like me. There are many men and women making bad choices everyday and are fated to experience serious financial setbacks sometime down the road. In my case I'd rather be single than choose incorrectly again.

I have never fully understood the rush to marriage in the United States. I've known people to get married after two weeks. Two weeks! What can you really know about someone in two weeks? What are their likes and dislikes? Does he leave the toilet seat up? Why do they leave bread crumbs on the sink? You should know these answers before you get married. You should know so much more.

One of my co-workers publically proclaims his intention to stay single for life. Although I don't fully support his position I understand it. I have to admire his tenacity too. He refuses to compromise his values or his expectations. He seems willing to wait out this life or the next until he finds the one he's looking for. How can you not appreciate his spirit?

You must understand waiting for RIGHT mate is something WORTH waiting for. The world is loaded with people who'd wish they had done just that. There are more single parents today than there has ever been. You should think about that before you rush to the altar. Statistics say 50% of marriages will end in divorce and some statistics predict 70% of second marriages will end in divorce too.

I'm hitting you with these statistics not because I'm anti-marriage. On the contrary I wish happiness and healthy relationships for all of us, including me. But I cannot ignore the stark reality of divorce and it would be irresponsible of me not to warn you of the pitfalls of short engagements.

Psychologists describe the period of infatuation as being anywhere from three months to three years. After this period is over your affection matures into something less-lustful but more deep and meaningful. You finally achieve true companionship. Don't fall for lust. Your feelings may very well be coming from your heart but scripture warns us that the heart is easily deceived. Stop and think! What do you really have to lose from a long engagement anyway? If there's any pressure at all from either party; I contend you don't have real love.

There is more than just relationship love there is "family" love and it feels so different. Family love is a deep devotion to the ones that always seem to be there for you. If you love your families ask them to purchase this book and the others on my reading list in later chapters. The teachings will provide them practical wisdom covering more than just money; the teachings provide wisdom covering life.

Chapter 16

In my youth I stressed freedom, and in my old age I stressed order. I have made the great discovery that liberty is a product of order.

-Will Durant

Money and your family

We are a society of consumers. We spend everything we get. I think we are that way because of a combination of nature and nurture. Most of our parents know very little about how money works so the chips are stacked against us from the start. From a young age we see very little saving and a whole lot of spending. It is a depressing sight to see and just like Flash-back TV, I keep seeing rerun after rerun.

If consumerism isn't taught at home by a child's biological parents, the kid's other parent takes over. I'm talking about television. Today it seems kids watch more television than ever before and the tube comes at them with a steady barrage of marketing all day long. If it isn't McDonalds; it's Mattel. If it is not Pixar; it's Disney. The list goes on and on.

Once I tried teaching my two young children about money. I ordered prepaid debit cards and I loaded each card with $20 a month. It was a futile effort. My daughter spent her allocation seemingly the minute it was loaded. My boy was excited about this newfound financial power and spent the cash as fast as it came to him too.

Frustrated and loaded with anxiety I pondered what to do. After being raised with a poor person's mentality, I stressed because I knew what was at stake. If I knew then what I know now about twenty years ago; I'd be a millionaire already. Although I have hundreds of thousands my poor person's understanding of money has held me back. I don't want that for them.

One day I loaded my boy into the car to drive him to school. With a sigh I looked at my son and wondered about his future. I wondered if he'd be frugal or a spender. I wondered if he'd make wise decisions about choosing friends and a mate. I exhaled deeply attempting to blow all the stress away.

I fumbled with a small storage compartment in my car between the passenger and driver's side seats. Absentmindedly I popped open the lid and stared at the black CD case inside. With curiosity I lifted the CD closer to my eyes and read the words out loud.

I said with interest "The Richest Man in Babylon by George S. Clason."

My boy swiveled in his seat. My words caught his attention.

I said "This CD is called The Richest Man in Babylon; it is really good." "Do you want to hear it?" I questioned.

He exhaled deeply. It was as if I asked him to take out the trash or something. "Sure." He replied indifferently.

I put the CD in the player and immediately the reader worked his magic. He skillfully varied his pitch, rate and pronunciation. His words captivated the listener and exploited the imagination. You really felt like you were in ancient Babylon during the reading. You smelled the stink of the overcrowded streets and felt the wetness of the camel sweat. You winched from the aroma of body order from the throngs and throngs of people sweating under the sweltering sun.

The storyteller was in impressive form and my boy hung on every word. I knew a breakthrough occurred when he started to ask questions about how money worked.

Now all I listen to are audio CDs about money in the car. I listen to them on the way to work. I listen to them when I pick up my boy from school. I listen to them during long drives. I listen to them during short ones. A steady barrage of financial wisdom has worked to educate my kids about money where the prepaid debit cards didn't.

My kids now budget intensely. In fact they use an excel spreadsheet that comprehensively tracks their cash flow. My kids log every purchase. I see them becoming more and more prepared for the real world and I am quite pleased.

You can never learn enough about money. I'm 38 years old and I've been investing for years but every day brings a new lesson. I'll never understand how someone can spend hours talking on the phone daily but they can't seem to find the time to devote one hour weekly to their personal finances.

I cannot stress the word frugality enough. If you want to be rich someday there's probably no word more important. According to Dictionary.com, the word frugality means "thrifty, chary, provident and careful." For the life of me I'll never understand why this word carries so many negative connotations. Most people choose to replace the word frugal with a more negative word like "cheap." I've been called cheap many times. It goes in one ear and quickly out the other. I suppose our culture of consumerism is what drives people's thoughts about being frugal. Many people replace the word frugal with cheap; I prefer to replace it with "wise."

There are so many "things" to buy in this country. No man or woman can buy them all. Therefore you must carefully consider EVERY purchase if you want to have money available to work for you. It you spend all you make there is no chance you'll ever experience financial freedom and you are sentencing yourself to work until you die. That is a terrible cross to bear.

As parents it is our responsibility to lay the financial foundation our children will need to be successful. It is a great responsibility perhaps our greatest besides teaching them right from wrong. Understand what's at stake if you fail in this responsibility. You are sentencing your children to financial slavery. They will carry a burden of debt no different than the burden the slaves carried when they built this country, centuries ago. Even when the slaves were free; they really were not. Sharecropping was a form of economic slavery forcing "free-men" to work from sun up to sun down for the rest of their lives.

All across America, from the ghettos to suburbs, economic slavery still exists. Consumer debt is the overseer. Debt keeps one going out the door to work and the minute you stop to ask for a break the whip cracks and you are forced to continue working.

I think of my mom bless her heart. At 62 years old previous debts continue to control her but I admit their hold on her is becoming less and less as she pays them off, one by one. We must all seriously take part in the struggle against debt and master it and money instead of these entities mastering us. It starts at home. Lessons taught there last a lifetime. If you teach your children convincingly they'll continue your teachings by teaching theirs. Your philosophy will last for generations. Teach your children. Teach your children traditional values, controlling desires, frugality and investing. If you do that the dollars you earn today will work for your children and your children's children for generations to come. You will demonstrate your love for them in the ultimate way; by leaving them assets to work for them until the end of time.

Chapter 17

I always laugh when people praise me as an overnight success. Overnight plus nine years of training, sacrifice, hard work and discipline was more like it.

-Mary Lou Retton

Taxes

The very word makes my blood boil. There is no subject that sets me off more than taxes. There is a legitimate reason for this too. It's not that I don't care about those less fortunate than me; it's just I don't feel the redistribution of wealth helps anyone. This is especially true for the very people redistributing wealth intends to help, the poor.

The poor are poor because their thinking is wrong. There isn't any other reason. It's not because of their environment. It's not because of their schools. The blame rests solely with them and GOVERNMENT cannot fix this. It must be fixed by personal responsibility. It is the only way. What happens when you give someone something for free? Let's get more specific, what happens when you give someone money for free? Do they appreciate it? Is it a one-time occurrence or do they come back asking for more money later? Does it bring the person you intended to help any lasting value? I tried to help someone once. It was a former girlfriend. She found herself stuck in a very bad situation. She took out an auto loan for several thousand at 18% interest. Can you believe that? 18%! The junky car was only worth a couple of thousand at most too. She was being exploited by the lending company. In a sense she was their slave.

So being a nice guy I offered to assume her loan since my credit is excellent and interest rates were ridiculously low. Instead of assuming the loan I decided to pay it off for her. I considered it a Christmas present. Overall she was a sweet girl and she'd do anything for me but she never appreciated what I did for her. We'd often talk about her finances and I offered advice on how to take control of her life. I tried to talk to her about the emotions of desire and a lifestyle of frugality since it was her ignorance of these subjects that got her in a bad situation in the first place but I was wasting my time. Everything went in one ear and out the other. This experience taught me an invaluable lesson; CHANGE MUST COME FROM WITHIN.

Overall there is an inherent goodness in people. We long to help those less fortunate than ourselves. Sometimes it's a family member; sometimes it's a complete stranger. I think back on my past and it is loaded with attempts to show good will towards people. I've donated money throughout my life to charity. I've given family members money. I've liberally given grants to friends. I've given to the homeless but through it all I've never really helped anyone.

There is an old story about a fisherman who was asked by one less fortunate for a free fish. Now this old fisherman was very wise and he knew if he gave away a free fish all that would happen is this person would come back tomorrow and ask for a free fish again. So the fisherman refused to give away a free fish and offered to teach this individual to fish instead. He offered to provide help in a way to promote independence not dependence. This is why I am so against high taxation and wealth redistribution. When you peel back the banana peel you aren't helping poverty by providing people things for free. To fully appreciate anything you must earn it through your own blood, sweat and tears! In other words you have deep appreciation for things you earn through your own labor. Brothers, girlfriends, sisters or mothers aren't helped at all when you just give them things. In fact YOU ARE DOING MORE DAMAGE TO THEM THAN YOU'LL EVER KNOW!

So I encourage everyone across this country to declare war on excessive taxation but let me be clear, I'm not advocating breaking the law or cheating on taxes. I'm advocating you take every legal means you can to minimize your tax burden. This reduces the amount of money available to the government to waste on worthless social programs that destroy personal responsibility, creativity, ingenuity and work ethic.

Let me give you an example of how excessive the tax burden is on the middle class. I'm going to use my own personal example because I have nothing to hide and I want to stick with real life examples as much as I can. This way you see what I preach is the truth and very applicable to real life.

In my profession I take home $6444.90 a month. That is $77,338.80 a year. I am considered middle class and I carry a heavy tax burden. I fall in the 25% tax bracket. Therefore a quarter of my income goes right to the government so they can build roads to nowhere or a silly fence along the border with Mexico. Or maybe the government will raise welfare benefits further encouraging laziness.

I grew up on welfare and I watched how self-destructive it is. You are provided everything through subsidies. We were given food, housing and spending cash without any real pressure to work. The effect on my mother was predictable. She chose not to work at all. She'd lay around the house counting the days until the next free check arrived despite being able-bodied and healthy enough for work.

She was an awful example for me and my siblings. Kids learn a lot from their environment so my brother dropped out of school early since he had no positive example at home and my sister didn't fare any better either. She dropped out by 16 years old and quickly rushed to get pregnant so she could get her free check too. I hope government officials wake up and smell the coffee because this is still going on today. Now back to my personal example. Assuming no deductions 25% or $19,334.70 of my income goes to the government to fund essential services like the military and a "ton" on unessential services like welfare, Pell Grants and others.

But I do claim some deductions so I'll use my real numbers. Let's start with federal taxes. My pay studs tell me $612.19 is deducted monthly for federal taxes. That's $7,346.28 a year and the government isn't done yet. My pay statement tells me $270.69 is taken for social security. That's $3,248.28 a year! That's a lot of money. That's a lot of money I could have invested for my own retirement but wait the government isn't done yet. Medicare takes an additional $93.45 every month. That's $1,121.40 every year. What's the grand total? From my middle class income the government takes

$11,715.96 a year. That's just like me working for the government for two months for free. There is no question why the middle class has eroded. It is because of heavy taxation.

Taxation to fight wars we don't need. Taxation for digging tunnels to nowhere and taxes for government grants to make fish smarter. Taxation for pork barrel spending that adds no lasting worth to the nation's economy or you or me. We would do so much better returning surplus money to America's citizens.

If we returned money to citizens they'd do one of two things with it. They'd either invest it or spend it. Either one of these options bring permanent value to America's economy. If they spend it consumers are purchasing worthwhile goods and services to enrich their lives. As demands for these goods and services increase businesses respond by hiring more people and creating meaningful jobs. What if consumers invest it?

Investing money provides capital every company needs to grow. This might materialize in a newly constructed McDonalds in your hometown or even critical research and development costs to discover a new prescription drug like Lipitor. In both of these scenarios the end result is the creation of meaningful jobs and new taxpayers. New workers for the McDonalds and new scientists for a pharmaceutical company like Pfizer. If Pfizer actually perfects a new medicine our economy benefits by adding additional manufacturing jobs due to a new product that is meaningful to us and the lives of people around the globe. What about the alternative point of view? What happens when the government grows and creates jobs in the government sector?

The answer to this question is "it depends." The results can be positive but past history is loaded with negative results. It depends on whether or not the jobs and the services they provide are useful. The government is notorious for creating too much redundancy and giving terrible customer service since it is nearly impossible to release government workers.

I recall I worked for over six months trying to resolve an issue with my child support. I was fully paid but the state of Texas had inaccurate data. I called every two weeks trying to resolve this and each time I was told my case was being worked and to call back later. All the while child support in excess of the court order was being garnished from my pay. It had a huge effect on my finances but the state government seemed not to care. I have examples of the federal government letting me down too with poor customer service and incompetence but the point is, if the services are useful to American citizens then growing government is beneficial but all too often the added jobs are worthless and add little to government efficiency and/or customer support.

I hope you're as mad as I am when you look at your pay statement. I hope you want to join me in my war against wasteful government spending and too much taxation. I hope you're ready to fight back. Now I'm going to show you how.

You must minimize your tax liability. This is crucial to grow wealth quickly. Let me show you how to do this. First you need to maximize contributions to your tax-deferred 401k program. In my personal example I can contribute over $16,000 a year to my 401k. This makes it seem like I only make $61,228.80 to the government despite actually making $77,338.80. This effectively limits my fair share of tax. Next you need to max out a Roth IRA if possible. A Roth is an individual retirement account designed to encourage saving for your retirement. You can open one through almost any financial institution. I like Vanguard. This is where I keep my own personal retirement account. At the time of this writing a single person can contribute up to $5,000 and its earnings grow tax-free. This is a good way to thumb your nose at the government and its high taxation.

Lastly you can take advantage of tax-free municipal bonds. These are loans to city and state governments. This strategy is more applicable to very high income earners. If you use this approach I'd accept some risk and go for the higher-yield municipals to maximize returns. There is greater risk here since these cities and states governments have had credit problems in the past but your risk is minimized somewhat by using a high-yield municipal bond fund. I'm sure in the worst case scenario these local and state governments will just raise taxes on their citizens to ensure you get paid anyway. Can you detect the bitterness I have on how citizens are treated and taxed in America? ☺

If you follow this strategy you'll get a fatter tax return at the end of the year. When that check arrives immediately buy new assets with it that produce income. In time your asset portfolio will grow and you'll be well on your way to significant riches and wealth.

In closing keep the government out of your pocket as much as you can. There is nothing patriotic about allowing the government to waste your money. In fact I argue it is more patriotic to limit your tax liability. If we all did this it would force politicians to finally make hard choices, eliminate budget deficits and tackle the national debt but right now politicians are under no real pressure thanks to indifference from the American taxpayer.

Chapter 18

Consider how hard it is to change yourself and you'll understand what little chance you have of changing others.

-Jacob Braude

Your values and the pursuit of money

Without one's values what does one have. I don't know who said that or I'd give him or her proper credit but it is profound. Money is power. I don't think anyone disputes that but it won't lead you to happiness. You must keep that in mind. As you start to accumulate wealth you'll need to fight off the human emotion of greed. If you can't control greed you are in danger of sacrificing your values of what is "right" in the pursuit of money.

I'll be the first to proclaim that it isn't worth it. Money is a means to an end but it should never actually define who we are. Money should be used for good not evil. A fool and his money is still a fool. I've seen money change people. Let's take my ex-wife for example.

I really thought I knew her. I'd brag about her unshakable resilience, strong values and exceptional conduct. In fact I didn't blame her or get incredibly angry when she asked for a divorced shortly after my return from Iraq. Even then I spoke highly of her but as time passed and the division of assets was brought up, she changed. Everything seemed all about her and what she could get out of the deal. From my point of view her children became less and less of a priority while money increasingly moved up the scale. She'd ask for more and more. Instead of two years spousal support; she now wanted three. Instead of two stock accounts she now wanted them all. For me it wasn't about the money. I told her I wanted to treat her fairly but it seemed to me she was infected by greed. Case in point, she even asked me to take out a second mortgage on the house so I could pay her more money. Can you believe that? The old wife I knew would have never approached me with that but this one did. She laid her cards on the table with no fear of folding. We'll just have to see how she turns out. Right now she lives in a big fancy house next to a judge. I hope that spousal support and the tens of thousands I gave her serves her well but I have a strong suspicion she is running out of money fast. In your pursuit of money don't ever sacrifice who you are. You may gain some money temporarily if you do but that money will never bring you any permanent value or happiness.

Money can bring out the best in people and the best in you. Let's suppose you invested wisely and were now sitting comfortably on several million in cash. What will you do with it? For most millionaires the prospect of creating more money through steady investment loses it luster. After you become a millionaire there's little gratification in earning additional millions. The only thing to do with the money at that point is to either spend it or give it away. Although plenty of people follow the first option and spend it; many others don't. Let's take Bill Gates for example.

Bill Gates is truly an exceptional American. He's the type of individual that comes around once every 100 years or so and we as a nation are very fortunate he was born in America. His contribution to our economic prosperity will be felt for decades to come since Microsoft Windows still remains the dominate operating system on over 92% of the world's personal computers at the time of this writing. At one point Bill Gates wealth exceeded $101 billion and he was listed as the second richest man in the world.

Yes, rightfully so Bill Gates is very rich. And yes, Bill Gates has many toys too. He has a 66,000 square foot estate complete with a 60 foot swimming pool with an underwater sound system. He has his own personal library and a custom dining hall that could easily feed a football team. His estate is so extravagant his annual property taxes alone are reportedly close to a million dollars a year. Yet I argue Bill Gates won't be remembered throughout history for his toys or his wealth. Those things quickly fade as time passes. Bill Gates will be remembered by his kindness to others.

In 1994 Bill Gates created the William H. Gates Foundation to deal with chronic problems affecting humanity across the globe. At the time of this writing the Gates Foundation has contributed $28 billion to charitable causes. The foundation is currently tackling chronic problems like immunizations in the third world and AIDS research. Other significant contributions are agricultural development and various programs to support and promote literacy and education. You see Bill Gates will largely be remembered for philanthropy not for Microsoft Windows. The goodness of Bill Gates wouldn't have been possible unless he was wealthy enough to allow it to bloom.

Wealth is not evil and the pursuit of money is worthwhile and good but some people become corrupted by its power and you must not let it happen to you. All across America every night, drug dealers take to the streets to peddle poison to their fellow man in the pursuit of money. These people do this in an effort to take shortcuts to wealth. They sacrifice their values and their salvation for a few dollars. Wealth acquired quickly and in this manner will never bring any permanent good to these people. In the end the money they acquire will eventually leave them as fast as water runs through a strainer. In the end these people will sit in jail cells wondering what happened to their lives. In other cases their lives will be cut short in a hail of gunfire somewhere in urban America.

Don't become corrupted by the pursuit of money. Don't ever sacrifice your values. You must always remember that you can't take money with you and when it is all said and done the only thing that really matters is whether or not it mattered that you were here. You will be judged by your goodness not your greed. There is no reason for short cuts either. Don't cheat on taxes in the pursuit of money. I know people who tried that and were caught by the IRS. A few extra thousand on a return almost turned into a jail sentence. Is your freedom really worth it? Don't lie to insurance companies to save some cash. Don't resort to crime or criminal behavior for a few bucks. Don't sacrifice who you are. Recall all the good values you were taught by your family or church and let them guide you in your decision-making. Rely on that inner voice that whispers to you when you are confronted by right and wrong. Let your conscience be your guide. If it feels wrong it probably is. You can acquire your fair share of wealth legally. There is abundance for all.

Chapter 19

Every small, positive change we can make in ourselves repays us in confidence in the future.

-Alice Walker

Desire, visualization and faith to achieve your goals

Without desire, visualization and faith you will never be rich or ever achieve any of your goals. Strong desire is fundamental. If the desire isn't there, you'll never want to be rich. If you don't desire financial security, you'll never have it. Most people scratch their head when I say that. The questions often arise "Doesn't everyone desire financial security?" "Doesn't everyone desire riches?" Sadly, the answer is no. There are plenty of people who talk the talk but never walk the walk. Just look around you. How many people talk about having a better life but don't pursue it? How many people talk about going to or finishing college but don't sign up for classes? How many people talk about wanting more money but don't take a second job? The truth is there isn't any desire there. Desire is the entity that gets you off the couch and moving. Desire makes you go to the college and sign up for classes. Desire is the force that makes you log on the computer and fill out job applications. Desire is an incredible power when one has it. It makes you accomplish things you never thought you could. You could lead massive organizations with strong desire if you want to. You can complete college in record time. I've seen it done. You can move mountains and swim oceans with desire. If you want to be rich you need to want it and I mean really want it. In the early 1990s I desired a college degree. I really wanted it. I wanted the esteem a college degree brought and I wanted to feel respected by my family. I pursued that degree with intensity. I really desired it. Despite challenges and setbacks I took college classes with what little free time I had. It was a breakneck schedule and I wouldn't wish it on my worst enemy but DESIRE got me through! Desire is the first step. It is a critical step and nothing else is possible without it. If you have no desire this book nor will any other book help you. Nothing will. You are doomed to a life of poverty and you will die with your full potential left sitting on the table.

The second concept I'd like to introduce to you is visualization. Visualization is the ability to see or imagine something. Most of the time, this is a future state. For you to become something, you have to visualize it. You need to see yourself as it. Suppose you want to be a doctor in the future. You need to visualize yourself in college. You need to visualize yourself in medical school. Finally you need to visualize yourself seeing patients. There is a curious quirk in the human mind. Your mind tries to achieve what it visualizes. Visualization works and you will succeed if you use it.

When I was a young enlisted man I'd visualize myself as a commissioned officer. I remember thinking it would be kind of cool to be saluted. I thought I'd make a good leader. So I started to visualize myself in college. I'd visualize myself getting a commission and I'd visualize myself leading troops. I still faithfully use visualization today.

I visualized myself writing this book. I've visualized myself owning real estate. I've visualized myself acquiring or starting companies. I've visualized myself as a respected parent and a loving father. I've visualized myself as a small business owner. Visualization works for many things and it is 100% reliable when used properly. You must start to visualize immediately. If you want to be a millionaire first desire it and then visualize it. It will happen if you do. You will become driven to achieve your goal. You will make better decisions motivated by the final end state. You will achieve it! You will creatively think of new ways to increase your cash flow! You will acquire newfound knowledge to move you towards your goal! Desire and visualization combined will open doors you never knew existed!

The last concept I'd like to introduce to you is faith. When I mention faith to someone they immediately think I'm coming at them from a religious angle. This is not the case. Faith is a strong belief in something. It doesn't necessarily mean a deity or some higher power but I'm not opposed to that approach if it works for you. Faith can simply mean just having faith in you. There are too many people conquered by their own self. Some people have no confidence in their own abilities. They may think they aren't smart enough. They may think they aren't pretty enough. They may think they don't have the energy to see a task through. They may think they simply don't have what it takes to compete with the other guy. These people just don't have faith in themselves. A lack of faith in one's own abilities is the key element holding one back. There are so many things just waiting for you to achieve if you only had faith in yourself. Mark Zuckerburg launched Facebook from a college dorm room because he had faith he would succeed!

Of course if you are deeply religious you can use faith in that manner too. Millions of people do it on a daily basis and make meaningful contributions to society and humanity. Religious faith has caused people to conquer incredible odds. History is loaded with plenty of examples of people accomplishing incredible feats with the power of religious faith. Norman Vincent Peale is a great American author and minister. He wrote a fantastic book called "The Power of Positive Thinking." From a small town boy to best-selling author, Mr. Peale is a shining example of the power of religious faith.

Chapter 20

The greatest pleasure in life is doing what people say you cannot do.

-Walter Bagehot

Continue to learn

This book is only a baby step. It was never intended to be a single source document. It's only the beginning. Refreshing and updating a person's financial and life skills must be a continuous endeavor. People and processes change, technology changes. The only way to stay current is seek out new knowledge and change with it. Although the concepts of financial management are as old as time; companies and products change. There will be new managers with new ideas and revolutionary lines of thought. Some managers will perform well, some won't. Some products will be fantastic and benefit mankind, some won't. You'll need to stay abreast on current developments through financial reports, magazines, books and websites. One can never have too much knowledge. Better yet you can never have enough wisdom and that is what good books and articles provide you. In my case I will never stop learning. My Kindle is loaded with financial books. I've got books from many authors advocating many different wealth growing strategies. These authors have shaped my own financial strategy. I have snatched a concept here. I have snagged a tidbit there. Financial wisdom is available for pennies on the dollar. The few bucks you pay for a good book will pay dividends pretty quickly once money starts working for you rather than you working for it. You'll realize different sources of income other than your salary. The following list contains books I've read. I think these books will further your financial and personal development. Some of these books cover more than just finance; they cover life. You will not only experience some creative writing but you'll experience a transformation in your thinking. You'll learn to treat others better and you'll develop a deeper understanding of money and life. This reading list is something I hope my most cherished family members will eventually read. I pray at one point they execute many of concepts preached by the writers in their own lives. I guarantee you'll be a better person from reading each and every one of these books.

I've decided to list the book and write a brief description on why I like it. This way you can really dig into the review before you decide to buy. All the listed books are best-sellers to my knowledge.

The Richest Man in Babylon: This book has been most influential in developing my own financial strategies. George Samuel Clason was a skilled writer and he used wonderful stories from ancient Babylon to illustrate financial concepts. The stories really support how financial concepts have changed little with time. This book is a work of literary art and its engaging stories are incredibly effective at introducing young children to financial ideas and money management. This is a must have book for anyone's library!

The Millionaire Next Door: The thing I got from this book is the importance of frugality and choices. Thomas J. Stanley and William D. Danko describe lifestyles of many of America's millionaires and their lifestyles don't fit our preconceived notions on now millionaires really live. There are no private jets, BMWs or mansions. These types of toys are for the super-rich. Common millionaires live in normal homes in working class neighbors. They drive used cars. This is an eye-opening book and after reading it you'll realize the folly of trying to keep up with the Jones.

Rich Dad, Poor Dad: This is a marvelous book based on the life and upbringing of the author, Robert Kiyosaki. The author tells a tale of having two dads. One was his actual biological father. The other was his friend's dad who acted as a cherished teacher, mentor and confidant to him. Both dads had their opinions and thoughts about money and investing and they were fundamentally different. The dads had different levels of financial success in life too. One died with millions while the other died with debts to pay. This is a great book that shifted my traditional thoughts on homeownership. It was the most valuable concept I snatched from this book and it shaped my current thoughts on the pitfalls of owning a home.

Men are from Mars, Women are from Venus: I'm sure many readers are scratching their heads wondering why I'd put a relationship book in here. The reason is this. So much of your accumulated wealth rests with your ability to have and grow meaningful, strong relationships with others. Too many people fail financially because their relationships fail. They end up going through costly divorces. Take my experience for example. I'm much poorer today due to a costly divorce. The divorce decree forced spousal support and a significant liquidation of my stock holdings cheating me out of years of compound interest and asset appreciation. I'm begging you to give equal attention to your relationships as you do to your quest to get rich. You can't have one without the other. This book may help you avoid some serious and costly financial setbacks along the way. The author, John Gray, is trying to help our relationships succeed; if only we'd accept his wisdom and help ourselves.

The Power of Positive Thinking: This book written by Dr. Norman Vincent Peale is an exploration in the power of an optimistic approach to everything. Dr. Peale is a well-known minister so naturally a lot of his concepts gravitate towards the Bible and its teaching. Nevertheless if you're religious or not I still recommend this book. The effect of positive thoughts on the human psyche cannot be denied. You will achieve more. You will have a more fulfilling life if you think positively. It is a well-documented fact and it is undisputed.

Think and Grow Rich: This is a personal development and self-help book written by Napoleon Hill. Although some spiritual references are mentioned in it; spirituality is not the focus of the book. It's more of a book on the power of faith and thought. This book formed my ideas on desire, visualization and faith. The catalog of famous Americans who have read and endorse this book is too big to list here. Many of America's most creative, successful people attribute a portion of their success to ideas discussed in this book. This is a must have, must read book along with the Richest Man in Babylon. Do not go without reading these two books. These books can change your life.

The Total Money Makeover: A Proven Plan for Financial Fitness: This is an entertaining book written by financial expert Dave Ramsey. The most important thing I got from it is my thoughts and belief on personal debt. Although I have used leverage in the past, Mr. Ramsey is

100% spot on in his assessment of the psychological aspects of owing someone something. Additionally his techniques on budgeting are the best I've seen. You will only come out ahead by reading this engaging book and you'll probably do like I did; I finished the whole thing in about four days.

That's all for my reading list. I'm sure in the future I'll have more. I fully believe education is a lifelong process. I think if one is to be successful it should never stop. The only time when it is acceptable to stop exercising your mind is when the lid closes on your coffin. The human brain is like any muscle. It requires regular exercise to perform at peak condition. I've been exposed to many people who stopped exercising critical thought years ago. They have no imagination. They have no creativity. Even the simple concepts in this book are too incredible for them to appreciate. These types of people will stay poor all their lives and there is no amount of government assistance that will change that. These people are poor in their thought and free money won't spark their transformation.

We live in a different age. At one point your local library was the only way to acquire knowledge. As a kid I had my own library card and I was a regular customer. I'd check out books on self-help and law. I'd check out fictional books to feed my vivid imagination. Those were good days but all good things eventually come to an end. The internet emerged in the 1990s and it was a game-changer. Since then I haven't been to a library in years.

The internet is a collection of linked computers for the purpose of sharing information. He who has the information has the power nowadays. Given that, there are several websites I'd like you to have to continue your growth. I use each one of them daily and I'd recommend the same for you. You will become a savvy investor much faster this way than trying to do it all on your own. I'll give you my recommendations just like I did with the books. I'll provide the web address and a brief description on why I think you'll like it. Here is the list below:

Yahoo! Finance - http://finance.yahoo.com/: I go to this website daily. The homepage lists a market summary showing you the overall pulse of the market. The headlines are the meat and potatoes. I quickly scan them for any articles of interest concerning my portfolio holdings. Use the quotes area to get more detailed information on your own holdings. On this site there are links to earnings release dates and economic calendars permitting you to track interest rates and indicators like new home sales. There is everything you could ever want on Yahoo! Finance and that's why I spend a lot time on it every day. Go ahead - Read some articles and surf around, I think you'll like what you find.

The Motley Fool - http://www.fool.com/: This is one of my favorite websites. It has a pleasing design and the articles are top notch and amusing. The Motley Fool CAPS feature is straight awesome! By creating a CAPS account which is free of charge you can create your own stock portfolio and track its progress. You'll see if you would've picked a winner or a loser. It is a marvelous way to learn about stocks without risking your own money. I needed to find this website twenty years ago. The community features are deep and appealing. You can see what other top rated investors are holding and sometimes they'll tell you why in a brief pitch. There are many features I love on this website but I won't bore you with details. The website is free. Go and check it out!

Investopedia - http://www.investopedia.com/#axzz1ZF92uL9G: Here is the place to go to learn about anything and everything finance. If you are introduced to a term during your quest for financial knowledge and you are unsure of its meaning, Investopedia will help. Additionally there are beginner's tutorials on this website to get you up to seasoned investor status in no time. There are opinion articles on the wisdom of renting vs. buying real estate and many other topics. There is more information on this site than you could dream of.

The Vanguard Group - https://personal.vanguard.com/us/CorporatePortal: The Vanguard Group is an investment and brokerage firm founded in 1975. It has $1.6 trillion in assets under management at the time of this writing. It is no doubt my most favorite brokerage company. The customer support is fantastic and their website is sleek and functional. On their website there are articles to increase your knowledge about money and investments. There are articles to help make sense of recently released economic indicators. There are articles written to provide support and encouragement during times of economic troubles. I use The Vanguard Group as my own brokerage company and I've done so since the mid 1990s. That was the first time I got involved in investing.

USAA - https://www.usaa.com/inet/ent_logon/Logon: USAA is a financial services company offering banking, insurance and investing services. Some services are only available to military personnel. A customer services representative can answer questions about which services are. At the time of this writing anyone can open checking and saving accounts through the company. I have all my banking and insurance accounts through USAA. I even used them for my mortgage loan. The customer service is excellent and the financial stability of the company is sound. If you don't have checking and savings accounts I'd recommend you look into USAA. If you already have these accounts elsewhere you may want to look at moving them to USAA. USAA has some of the lowest fees in the nation with the best features. For example if you withdraw money from a non USAA ATM your withdrawal fees are refunded by the end of the month. This is just one small perk of many that makes USAA stand out from the crowd.

Zillow - http://www.zillow.com/: At some point you'll want to buy a home and I think Zillow is the best place to find a good deal. The coolest feature is their patent Zestimate. It uses market conditions, home features and recent sales to estimate the value of a home. This feature can ensure you are paying a fair price considering comparable sales in the area. This feature can highlight homes selling significantly under market value too. I've used it myself in my real estate transactions as a starting point for negotiations on new purchases. It's free of charge but big on information for consumers.

Chapter 21

About ninety percent of the things in our lives are right and about ten percent are wrong. If we want to be happy, all we have to do is to concentrate on the ninety percent that are right and ignore the ten percent that are wrong.

-Dale Carnegie

Final thoughts

The quote above illustrates what is really important in life. If your quest for money is because you think money will bring you happiness, it won't. I have enough money to know that but if you pursue money as a tool to enrich your own life and the lives of others; you are going after it for the all the right reasons. Don't misunderstand me. Money is vitally important. It's imperative you claim your fair share of America's wealth. Just imagine an America where everyone did.

The crime rate would fall. Crime is an immoral act sometimes sparked by necessity. A woman needs to pay the rent so she resorts to prostitution to do it. A young father needs to pay the bills so he resorts to selling drugs. If only these people would listen to what I'm saying, live under their means and store wealth; they'd be okay.

My sister is a good example. She is using 38% of her disposable income just for rent. After I found about this I tried to help her. I explained to her that too much of her income was going to housing costs and I made the benefits of moving to a more affordable apartment clear. I explained that she'd have more disposable income for life's pleasures. She simply stared at me blankly. She shook her head from time to time in weak acknowledgement but it was clear to me she didn't grasp what I said. I tried a different approach. I talked about desire, visualization and faith. Again I was met with empty looks and blank eyes. The light never came on. Disappointed and dejected, for the time being, I gave up but it isn't over. In my mind, I lost one battle but I don't intend to lose this war. This is an example of how one can sentence their own self to voluntarily economic slavery. She has become so institutionalized in her line of thought she rejected freedom when the keys were offered to her. We, as a country, have many brothers and sisters struggling in this same state.

This book won't end poverty. The problem is too big for any one book but maybe, just maybe it can put a dent in it. If I can accomplish that, writing this book was well worth it. I set out to help those who have been ignored for many years. I set out to help the working poor with a roadmap to prosperity. It begins with you controlling your desires for material possessions and by exercising some self control. Budgeting and saving are key components and it all ends with harnessing your desire for something better, visualizing it and having faith in oneself.

The words above summarize this entire book in a nutshell. They are the gospel truth. I hope and I pray that everyone that reads this book starts to execute the concepts for better living immediately and they enjoy a more fulfilling and enriching life.

Message from the Author

First, thank you for reading this book. It is my greatest hope you had as much pleasure reading it as I did writing it.

Why did I write and publish this book? Originally, it was never intended for publication. I wrote it simply as a financial guide for my two children. I wanted to capture my experiences with money and pass this knowledge down to them. In a sense, I wanted to create a guide that would equip them for life. I hoped my kids would avoid my mistakes and replicate my successes. Why did I write this book? Ultimately, I wrote it for love.

Why did I publish it? In order to answer that question, you must learn a little about me. I am passionate about money and personal finance; I find the topics fascinating. It should come as no surprise; these subjects drift into my daily conversations.

One day, I had a chat about personal finance with a co-worker. I encouraged him to take positive steps to reclaim his life. I showed him simple techniques to control his spending, reduce his debts and save for the future. After a lengthy but rewarding discussion, he committed to do just that. We shook hands and said our goodbyes. As he parted, he turned and said "Hey, you should write a book." I found his words a twist of fate since I already had a personal finance book written. It simply sat on my shelf, helping no one. At that moment, I decided to publish it in order to help others.

I finished writing this book at the end of 2011. At that time, I had close to a half-million in assets. It is now 2013 and my asset tree has grown to $670,000. That's a 25% increase in just two short years. I am well on my way to becoming a millionaire, retiring early and living off the fruits of my asset tree. The tactics, techniques and procedures in this book work if you sacrifice and apply them.

Some people question my strategy of never, ever sell a stock. Should you never, ever sell a stock? It really depends. You should only hold great companies forever. These are hard to find but if you dig into a company's SEC filings; you will find some. Along with the other key statistics listed in this book, monitor their revenues, business strategy, inventory and same-store sales over time. These tidbits of data are great indicators of a company's past, present and future. Have I sold stocks in the past? Of course I have. Sometimes companies start off good but they lose their way. Sometimes companies lose touch with consumers. Sometimes companies fail to adapt to changing trends. However, if you wrap your arms around the best companies hold on and watch your wealth grow substantially over the years.

The encouragement I have received from my family and friends is invigorating. I cannot thank them enough for their kind words but I'm just like you and I can always use further support.

If you enjoyed this book, please review it on Amazon.com. Your encouragement is welcome and truly inspiring. Your kind words reassure me that my cause is just and my efforts are appreciated by those who matter most. Thank you again and I wish you good health. I hope you will achieve the personal and financial prosperity you seek.

                    Sincerely,
                    Kevin McNeely

Index

85% method, 49, 50, 53, 117
accounting, 2, 28, 30
Annual Report, 83
asset, 35, 36, 38, 39, 41, 71, 77, 93, 95, 98, 100, 107, 120, 154, 168
average annual return, 70
bonds, 37, 41, 60, 63, 68, 69, 70, 89, 90, 91, 153
budget, 31, 45, 57, 93, 110, 115, 127, 143, 154
capital, 44, 63, 67, 69, 71, 91, 95, 151
cash flow, 31, 32, 33, 35, 37, 49, 58, 65, 90, 110, 120, 143, 163
Certificates of Deposits, 59
consumer credit, 99, 100, 101, 110, 120
corporate bonds, 68
desire, 8, 14, 15, 16, 18, 51, 83, 95, 108, 112, 116, 147, 160, 162, 169, 176, 177
DIV & Yield, 72
Dividend yield, 72
dividends, 34, 68, 69, 71, 72, 79, 80, 88, 91, 97, 98, 100, 119
Exchange-Traded Funds, 118
expense ratios, 70
Family love, 139
FDIC, 51
FICA, 62
frugality, 143, 145, 147, 167
income, 8, 11, 12, 13, 21, 25, 32, 33, 34, 37, 42, 43, 50, 57, 62, 64, 65, 66, 69, 70, 71, 74, 75, 76, 78, 81, 90, 99, 100, 101, 103, 109, 110, 112, 114, 117, 118, 120, 123, 125, 126, 149, 150, 153, 154, 166, 176
income statement, 74
junk bonds, 42
Loaded funds, 70
minimum wage, 13, 21, 22, 23, 24, 28, 42, 65, 69, 71, 103, 108, 109, 112, 118, 125
Mutual funds, 68
operating costs, 70, 76
payout ratio, 72, 79, 80
price to earnings ratio, 72
principal, 37, 38, 65, 67, 77, 82, 87, 95, 97, 127
Quarterly Report, 83
return on assets, 76
return on equity, 76, 77
run on banks, 51
saving account, 59, 60
Securities, 60, 83
Self-service, 52
shareholders, 79, 80
Social Security, 61, 62, 63
stocks, 37, 40, 67, 68, 69, 71, 72, 74, 75, 76, 77, 81, 83, 88, 89, 90, 91, 97, 100, 118, 172
Suggestion, 19
total revenue, 74
Valuation measures, 71
vision, 83, 93, 111
wealth, 8, 9, 10, 11, 13, 25, 27, 28, 33, 37, 38, 43, 46, 66, 90, 93, 102, 103, 110, 111, 117,

119, 128, 146, 148, 153, 154,
155, 157, 158, 159, 166, 176

www.ingramcontent.com/pod-product-compliance
Lightning Source LLC
Chambersburg PA
CBHW051652170526
45167CB00001B/430